let *Love* LIVE

by Shirley Crews Taylor

A Collection of Love Poems
Volume II

Published by: SAC Creations

                 P O Box 720464

                 Houston, TX 77272

Cover by: Kbizz Solutions

ISBNs
Paperback: 979-8-9936674-1-6
Ebook: 979-8-9936674-0-9

Printed in the United States

by Shirley Crews Taylor

Acknowledgements

For acknowledgements, I have to start with my Aunt Daisy Dobynes and my mother Mildred Ann Crews. Aunt Daisey was larger than life in her personality and all she embodied. She had a fire and zest for life that I am forever changed by the opportunity to witness in this lifetime. In the year before she passed, we were able to reconnect and it truly blessed my life. I had just lost my dad and my mother was very ill. She called to give her condolences and to support me. My mom passed away about a month later. She later told me that she was very ill as well. We continued to speak by phone, and eventually she invited me down for a visit. It was such a life changing, paradigm shifting time. After I shared my first book with her about love and relationships, she said I love this book because I love you. But where are your poems about God? I explained that I had a personal relationship with God. She was a pastor and had very strong beliefs. I was not a person that thought I did not have to share what I believed, but thought it would show from what others saw in me. I also struggled with being accepted and never wanted to alienate anyone because I knew the hurt of rejection. I have vowed to let Love Live and to always choose love. This caused me to spend some time reflecting on my beliefs and sharing my voice. I wrote a poem called "That Melton Pride" which is in this book and shares more about our experience. Well Aunt Daisey, here is my book about inspiration, self exploration, faith and God. I hope it will inspire others like you have inspired me to share my story.

About my mother, Mildred Ann Crews, where do I start? There are so many life lessons that came from being her daughter. She was a proud, strong woman and raised me to be strong. Her courage and grace in life and death has had a

profound effect on me. I thank her for all of her sacrifices and love for her only biological daughter and all the children she raised as her own. After my mom's passing, I felt I had to grow up, to mature spiritually and emotionally. I had no idea what stock I came from until after she passed. Her family showed up in droves. They called, prayed, sent letters and just surrounded us with support. I am so thankful for the family and DNA that I share as well as the support that I discovered I did not know I needed. Through all of my experiences in my journey, the ups and downs, I am learning to trust myself. I was a very shy girl and until recently, I did not understand the power of my own voice and that there was room for me to be just the way God made me. I had to learn to stand on his promises to be able to see the gifts and talents in myself to become the woman that I am today.

My experiences with limited mindsets, depression, and self-doubt caused me to stay in the wilderness for far too long. But, I am thankful for grace, renewal and healing. I had to decide if my writing for this book would be a sad story or a testimony. I now know that it is a testimony. I pray that sharing my vulnerabilities and struggles to be my authentic self will help someone else to be resilient and exhibit grace to themselves on this journey called life.

I dedicate this book to my husband George who continues to encourage me to write and share my gift with others. Thank you George for always believing in me and my dreams. To my son Gheori and my daughter Sydney who inspire me daily to be my very best. Your unconditional love helps me understand what real love is all about and motivates me to keep going.

I was thinking about the women (friends, sisters) that have stood in the gap with me. Taking my calls when I could not speak, lifting me up when I was down on myself. I thank you for the many prayers and positive energy from friendship, sisterhood, brotherhood, and for unconditionally love when I did not have it for myself. As I put the finishing touches on my book, I have to thank all of my friends and family who have believed in my dreams and vision before I could fully realize them for myself. Many thanks to all of those who always support me in my many endeavors and have influenced this project in some way.

INTRODUCTION

I am embarking on an adventure and I invite you to join me. This book of poetry entitled, "Let Love Live" Volume II includes poems about biblical verses, spirituality, inspiration, self-exploration and finding our way through the transition and flow of life.

In my journey, I have come to appreciate my lessons to develop resilience and to inspire hope in others through sharing my writing. It has not been easy. I have finally found the courage to share my story. My transformation has not been a smooth transition, but filled with limiting mindsets, depression, despair and strength to rebuild again and again.

It has not been easy to be honest and authentic with yourself and open with others. My life experiences have not been anything to write home about or so I thought. I often felt different and through my isolation I fed my spirit information that was not always helpful and nurturing. In my writing, you will see threads of depression, low self-esteem, excessive doubt, and a woman that was often unsure of herself. But, through God's grace I am still here. I am a work in progress as we all are as we navigate our lives. I am also excited to share that my writing also includes stories and poetry about growth, overcoming and dispelling untruths that somehow entered my spirit. I thank God for my healing and the many lessons that I have learned. I thank him for allowing me to find support through the encouragement of others and for their genuine unconditional love for me. I could name names, but the important fact that I would like you to take away from this collection of short stories and poetry is that no matter how challenging our day-to-day lives can become, there is always hope.

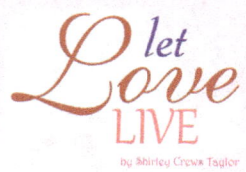

let
Love
LIVE
by Shirley Crews Taylor

Self reflection and exploration is an important part of the healing and the growth process. You have to know who you are, what you truly believe in and to have the courage to stand on that apologetically. In this book, "I said what I said!". In today's "Cancel Culture", it can be difficult to be authentic and speak your heart freely. This collection of poetry comes from years of just living and trying to be my best self without the resources, tools and some misinformation. Each year that I have been blessed to see another day, I am encouraged because I know I have another chance to try my best to show love to myself and others.

In those quiet hours, I could hear what my spirit and God was sharing with me. I allowed myself to let the words flow freely onto the page without censorship or judgment. I was amazed. In my efforts to find strength and courage to aspire to have the desires of my heart, I have often fallen short. We all fall short in certain areas of ourselves, and finally for me it is ok to make mistakes and not be a people pleaser. I have discovered that we all need connection and belonging as human beings. I finally found my tribe.

I have been fortunate to carve out my own path, and for this I am grateful. Although, this is not the end of my story, and I know there will be more missteps, as well as triumphs, but I am here for it. I am finally present in my own life. I no longer hold my past against myself, and do not focus so much on the future. I strive to stay in the moment, and it is a challenge, but when I find myself drifting away, I kindly return to me. I am practicing giving the same grace to myself that I so freely give to others without asking. I hope my sharing will encourage you to do the same.

My narrative was sometimes written with the lenses of uncertainty and renewal in spirit. In my quiet times, a gentle nudge pushes me to love myself, go for my dreams, and provides an unwavering desire to live my purpose of encouraging the hearts of others.

I invite you to commit to personal development, and exhibiting grace when you do not feel your best about you or your current situation. I have included a few bible verses that have encouraged my spirit when I needed it. Thanks to my Aunt Daisy, I am sharing that side of my spiritual writing in my work.

So, here we go, entering into the next pages of my thoughts and feelings scattered throughout this book for the world to see and feel. I hope that you will be able to "feel me" on every page and that God will bless it so that it touches the hearts and spirits of others that need it most.

I have included blank pages for you to capture your thoughts as you ponder the words of each poem and allow your heart to speak.

"This book is for everyone who has ever struggled with their faith, confidence, self-love, self-doubts and the courage to be your authentic self."

let
Love
LIVE
by Shirley Crews Taylor

Table of Contents

Chapter one

In Wake of New Emotions

Chapter Two

Inspirational Stories of Healing and New Starts

Chapter Three

For the People I love

Chapter Four

Beneath the Surface Embracing Self Love

Chapter Five

When the Heart Speaks

Chapter Six

Echoes of Everyday Love

Chapter Seven

Encouragement for the Journey

Chapter Eight

Prayers and Verses

by Shirley Crews Taylor

My Vow To Let Love Live Too!

"Every since I took that vow to "Let Love Live" Everything has popped off, and life has been all uphill Bitterness and resentment started to kick in

In today's climate, I was at my wits end

Responsibility and being a good person became a bad word,

My spirit has been so loud and chaotic that I could not hear God's word I thought I could inspire others with inspiration and guidance

But my spirit became filled with unforgiveness and defiance

I had to take some time to reflect on what letting love live really meant I can say that my time in reflection has been time well spent

Love has not changed, and it is still a verb and action

I will Let Love Live too, and not give haters the satisfaction So, I am back on my grind and letting my light shine

Continuing to encourage the hearts of others and to myself be kind"

In the Wake of New Emotions

Sometimes emotions can be so raw and painful that you just shut down and numb yourself to all emotions, both good and bad. For me, I chose to do the work and experience all of the emotions that became too much. I had to be open to feel again and to keep moving. Trust the process.

Open

My senses are open again, I feel so alive and renewed,

Emotions are light and thoughts are no longer skewed...

Towards negativity and limitations from the past

A new dawn has come and I want this feeling to last

Even my sense of smell is sharper and I can finally hear

My inner most thoughts and the sound of love ringing in my

ear I am aware of my body and the woman that I have become

The taste is so sweet, I recommend whatever
this is that you have some

I can see clearly now, and even though
I was always a woman with vision

I am no longer waffling, but very confident with every decision.

Reaching Out

Sometimes you get caught up with the day-to-day, and the messages are always so strong that you forget to stop and pray. You can push yourself to be driven that neglect can set in and you lose connection. Oftentimes, we look to friends and family to feed our spirit but they are pouring from an empty cup themselves. It is in those times when your soul and spirit is reaching out, but nothing works. This is the place where you can get to the point of surrender.

I am reaching out because the heart is searching
For the relief of the loneliness and all the hurting
Now, I am willing to make efforts to be
vulnerable for what daily I seek
So I put pen to paper and let the words leak the words and emotions
coming from my spirit
Reaching out so someone that cares for me and might hear it…
Longing for the connection I do not have and not sure how to find
Pushing down thoughts of how to get what I need
But it seems my heart and the hunger I cannot feed
So for now I keep searching but I must admit to losing hope and
desperation is sinking in
I am getting careless and throwing caution to the wind 🧡

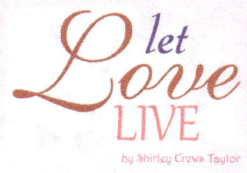

Make A New Start

You have to be able to get out of your head and stay out of your own way. As I would ponder the questions and find the answers that I was seeking, I would get frustrated. When I felt like I was doing my best, but my best was not good enough, it affects your resilience and can dampen your hopes and dreams. But you have to find the courage to keep going, to be kind to yourself and focus on the small victories that really matter when you feel that you are not making progress.

Sometimes I get so angry at myself when it seems like I am waiting
around for someone to feed me or throw me a bone
I mean I am furious, I am tired of being
strong,and feel so all alone
That saying have your people call
my people is so tired and weary
Trying to build your own path and be
authentic can be so challenging and scary
I often wonder who really has my back
Who out there will cut me some slack
Then it comes to me that at times
all you can depend on is the God in you
In those times you might not know what to do
You seek others for guidance but, they can't see your vision
It seems like everyday you are
asking someone else for permission
During those times I have to dive deep and say

Let
Love
LIVE

by Shirley Crews Taylor

"Will the real Shirley Crews Taylor please stand up!"
When the Christ in you is buried so deeply,
and you are pouring from an empty cup.
But, then it comes to you that God is our source and I am thankful for his grace
I pull myself together (again) to find the courage to tackle whatever I need to face
It is frustrating when you give all you've got to give
that you start to doubt the desires of your heart Take the time to regroup, knowing you are worth it,
and find the courage to make a new start.

Hindsight

I find myself sitting here thinking about
my life and my journey thus far
The highs the lows the joys the scar
The challenges as a shy black girl
Looking back it was such a small world
I don't remember anyone telling me that
I could be whatever I aspired to be
My vision was so limited and I just couldn't see
All of the great qualities that I was blessed to have inside and out
I was too hard on myself and would later
learn what self love was all about.
They say hindsight is 20/20, but how was I to know
What I was capable of and that my light was ok to show?
I don't remember anyone saying to
hide my light and not speak your mind
But when I searched my spirit there
were hidden messages and hard to find
Now I am learning just taking it day by day
Knowing that though I might stumble I would find my way

Unspoken Fears

"I have often found myself wrestling with uncertainties just beneath the service and I cannot always put my finger on it. I sense that something is not right within my spirit. I wrote this poem because I just know that I was not the only one experiencing feelings of doubt and fears, but did not recognize it. Sometimes, it creeps into your mind and spirit from simple ideas, conversations that begin to collect and build doubt. I hope you will take the time to become more self aware and cleanse regularly what no longer serves you and is limiting your life."

What is this unspoken fear that is holding you captive
That thing that is blocking you from
living the life you so want to live
Do you even know and can you identify what is what
Or is just a sick feeling deep down in your gut
Does it come on strongly every time you are ready to make that
move or take a chance
Does it stop you every time you want to advance
Are you self-sabotaging and blocking your blessing
Does it break your sleep and have you stressing
Does it cause you to be numb and instead of facing
your fear you run
Or are you standing firm and saying to fear this time you're done
Can you even look yourself in the face
Or is distraction keeping you from the goals that you chase

When you try to express this unspoken fear are you frozen and mute Are you finally ready and wanting to give your fear the boot Are you willing to fight to be successful and push through your fear Will you do it today right now right here...

Unspoken Fears.

Up Again At Three

Eyes wide open with thoughts of yesterday haunting me
Negative thoughts and past conversations held me hostage again
Just when I thought I was getting better and on the mend
This time it was a phone call with a message that I did not expect
Like a thief it snatched my joy and filled me with regret
I tried to shake it like a boxer who can bob and weave
But that's what I get for wearing my heart on my sleeve
I had to go deep within myself and use some positive self talk
How no matter what it was,
I still have value and that it wasn't my fault.
Most of the day it felt like a lie
I even felt like I wanted to cry
I tried calling a friend but they did not answer the call
I admit I tried to reach another friend,
and on my knees to God I did not fall
Again, no answer by this time the
pain is so great I finally think to pray
 Knowing God already knew my situation and what I had to say
It is usually something simple, like "God, please help me!"
I waited until I could take all I could take before I would
surrender and break free How many of us do not stop
to pray as our first line of defense
Do you wait like me once you've lost all sense

I know the Serenity prayer but not sure what is within my control
I keeping allowing everything deep down into my soul
So thankful for prayer and each day to try to be a better me I will
resist the thoughts that will have me up again at three

by Shirley Crown Taylor

What Came Up

I have gone through life trying to keep the peace and to be humble. I often raged a silent war inside of myself that shaped my inconsistencies of not standing on what I believed. I have often been lost in this journey and have not been certain of who I was and what I believed. My struggles with depression, limited thinking, outgrown beliefs and lack of confidence have spilled out over my life. Sometimes, I felt alone, I was losing hope and I had not found my voice. I thought I had to go along to get along and not speak my mind, especially when there was the potential for conflict and misunderstanding. But, not speaking my heart and allowing myself to be and become how God made me left me wrestling with emotions that overwhelmed me daily. I thank God for my healing.

Sometimes I try to contain all the emotion and not let them flow
But the pressure builds so heavy it feels like I'm about to blow
Holding down feelings so deep
Thoughts that linger and won't let me sleep
Ideas banging around in my head
To verbalize them I'd rather do anything else instead
So I tighten the lid on the woulda shoulda coulda and must
Especially all the societal rules and other sins like lust
I wrestle with feelings with no words so I toss and I turn
I want to be understood so badly and how my heart does yearn...
For love, acceptance and connectivity
Man I just wanna live and let live —
know what it feels like to be free.

The Morning I Woke Up To Tears

This morning I woke up to tears

The bow finally broke from the pressure over the years

You see from the pain, I was totally numb

And now with all of the pressure I've finally succumb

You know I've been waiting for my breakthrough

From all the hard work I thought it has been long overdue

I've been praying and agreeing seeking the desires of my heart

But nothing has happened yet, and no one can say
I haven't done my part

For as long as I can remember I had my hustle on

Now it seems like the years and time
I don't know where they've gone

The tears are definitely sadness,
but I must say there's a lot of anger inside

let Love LIVE
by Shirley Crews Taylor

I am now so disillusioned that the disappointment,
I can no longer hide

I've used positive self talk and mantras but it was all BS

I am truly buckling under the stress

People asked me girl where is your faith have you lost all belief

No, but it's been overshadowed with heartache and grief

Yes, after years, the tears finally came,

and I won't look at my dreams or people ever the same

I know I can't give up so I'm just going to
have my moment and let the tears flow

I hope to find joy and strength again it's
just been hard to let it all go

Something's Bothering Me

Something is bothering me but I can't put my finger on it

I will sit here and ponder on it a bit

My whole life is in complete disarray

My time had been all work and no play

Am I burned out again

On whom can I really depend

My body is hungry for things that alone I can't fulfill

Maybe I need a win and I just to get quiet and be still

What Disappointment Feels Like

There are times in life no matter who you are will go through trials and your path gets labored. I have often found myself lingering in frustration because things were not happening on my desired timeline. People and situations were not cooperative and my world was filled with darkness. I often dimmed my light. Each day can make you weary with the weight of responsibility, hopes and dreams. You wonder, "when prayers will be answered and dreams realized?" You find a way to pull yourself together and search for comfort during this season of life.

How do you deal with disappointment in man and humanity
The pain of it all leaves me frustrated and feeling no sense of unity
 I sit on the side of my bed as the tears fall into my coffee cup
The pressure feels so heavy that it's hard to look up
I have tried to do what was required and play my role
But broken promises and unmet expectations have hurt my soul
As the tears flow I realize I am exhausted as my heart does break
I don't know how to get what I need and
I don't know how much more that I can take
I've gotten lost on this journey again
To be honest I can't remember how the disappointments began
I guess it was as a little girl when people said

let
Love
LIVE
by Shirley Crews Taylor

they would do things that didn't come through
Or others betraying me and telling me things
that just weren't true
Oh let's talk about love and how we all need
to be wanted and cared about
How do signals get twisted and you end up with pain and doubt
Or me trying to follow the rules and traditions of society
Not knowing how to be authentic and truly free
Why do I have such a sensitive spirit to everything around me
I can feel the hurts of others so strongly deep in my soul
It's hard to shake and has such a stronghold
This is what disappointment feels like and
the tears make it hard to see
Lord help me

let
Love
LIVE
by Shirley Crews Taylor

If I Didn't Tell You Today

When I think of you, it tends to bring a smile

You still have that youthful spirit and an easy going style

I still ponder what is the life lesson for our reconnection

Not sure why, but I am thankful for the kindness and affection.

We've had a chance to do a review of past relationships,
and share our present life today.

I hope that what I have done or added something
of value in some way

Your friendship and encouragement is appreciated
if I didn't tell you today.

Misery

Misery, like convincing myself I can have it all my way
I must be tripping because I keep ending up in
that space almost every day
The dictionary defines misery as "a state or feeling of great
distress or discomfort in the mind or body"
This can happen a lot when you are "trying to be somebody"
Especially if life constantly tries to convince
you that you're not (somebody)
Not to mention when things don't work out
even when you've given it all you've got
Thoughts can make you think you are invincible
Then you find yourself doing the unthinkable
The mind can play some tricks on you if you let it
Can talk you into doing things you don't normally
do and you'll regret it
Imagination can get you confused with reality
and you can't tell which is which
Man I tell you life can be a real son of a ...
Misery is like trying wear shoes two sizes too small
Telling yourself you would only have a bite but then you at it all
It makes you forget to be thankful, grateful,
appreciative or ever satisfied
You focus on what you can't do or don't have
and it kills all joy inside
So why do we end up in misery and choose to stay
Because real change can be harder than thinking this way.

Suddenly

I sit here this morning taking a break from cleaning my house
I think about my life with kids and a spouse
The complexities of relationships and why people stay
How things can go unnoticed for years and you are
now uncertain how they got that way.
Until something happens to get your
attention and you can view life through new lenses
You finally awake and can feel all of your senses
Things look new, fresh but a lot of things look old and tattered
Your mind has been all over the place and your thoughts are
scattered. You woke up each morning just trying to get through
the week
Who knew the many years that would pass
so quickly on the journey you seek.
Where did the time go and what about the dreams you had?
Its like you have a pile of memories some happy others sad
Things suddenly drifted out of control like a fire with a little wind
You look back to assess the situation
but you don't know where to begin
It seemed like you managed to stay in the
house and missed a beautiful day
You missed many opportunities to say what you had to say
Before you let it overwhelm you, you gather your thoughts
and find your way back to reality and try to be grateful
That you get to see another day and the chance to try again...
for that you are thankful.

Restlessness...A Mood

I can't find a comfortable spot in my mind or my
seat I'm tossing and turning unsteady on my feet
The thoughts rush in and I physically fight back the fear
I think to myself what a heck of a year
The pandemic ... hurricanes... election year and I must vote or die!
The frustration, anger and anxiety runs high
I feel clingy and want to hoard everybody I love as my hope fades
The politicians messing around having scandals and escapades
People are losing their lives and some think it's just a game
All I can say is what a shame what a shame what a shame
Sending our kids back to school they got to learn
This social distancing got me waiting my turn
But what the heck for because everything is selling out
Like the Gap band makes me want to shout
But I can't give up and that's what's real
But it's hard to change the way I feel
Covid got me can't even get a hug
Not trying to push this under the rug
Watching the news got me ready to start packing
If anyone get out of line I'm about to start (capping) smacking
So... now that I got that out my system its back to minding
my own biz and finding me a snack
But, I don't care what anybody say my year was whack
Now run tell that...

I Am Sad Y'all

I am just sad y'all
I usually try and stand tall
But this time I am going to sit in this feeling
to see what it is really about
I feel like crying and might even shout
I am not going to self medicate
I would usually eat something sweet like cake
No, I am going to sit here and feel the raw emotional pain
I know not to stay too long and drive myself insane
But, just for a time I won't run or find some distraction
I will ponder my thoughts and the cause of dissatisfaction
I know God is able and I really do pray
I am getting quiet to see what he has to say
So don't worry if I don't answer my phone for a while
Please don't think that I am acting funny
when you do not see me smile
I am just sad y'all…

Change My Luck...(My Blessing—Stop Stressing!)

When I try to think and live with a heart of love...
I am stopped dead in my tracks.
With negativity, bitterness, regrets, anger...
and everything that I lack.
To create a list of what is wrong, I can write all night.
I only hear crickets when I have to identify what's right.
I call it "melancholy", my counselor says it is depression.
Either way, I keep repeating the same life lesson.
What does God want me to do and why do I have to guess?
Ladies, yes, I know... I am a hot mess!
The taste of disdain runs powerful through my veins...
Who can I really talk to; where can I share.
I feel I am just screwed up and no one really seems to care!
I try to talk to Jesus, but I sometimes can't find the words to express. And the people on earth sometimes it seems that they can care less!
So I feed off of bought affection and suck
up any attention that I can get.
I walk around every day, thinking nobody gets me yet.
I can't bring myself to say forget it and just give up I pray every day that something will change my luck

Reflection Page
Chapter 1

_____

_____

_____

_____

_____

_____

_____

_____

_____

_____

Inspirational Stories of Healing and New *Starts*

The seasons of my life as I maneuver though my journey, I am thankful for the glimmer of hope and the silver linings. I have had so many storms in life with depression and general struggles of day-to-day. The healing and new starts have come in phases and I am appreciative and grateful for the many lessons.

Fresh and Deep
From the Soul Series

Attention! Attention! Hey guys listen up!
I finally have something to say, ready to spill my cup
I have been doing the work ,and the layers have shed like hair
I've gotten past the injustice and how life isn't fair
I went deep and did not stop when I felt pain
I knew if I could push through it there would
be so much more to gain
I picked up my pen, I talked it out with a friend
The words and thoughts began to flow and the pieces fell into place
I realized that I was in charge of my life and could set the pace
I ran for so long and was deep in distraction
But my misery and discontent lead me to take action
The teacher showed up when I was ready to learn
I finally stepped up and took my turn
I forgave myself and replaced with love those
places where I and others had damaged myself
I took my dreams from the back burner and off the shelf
I went to the mirror to get a glimpse of the real me
So this is what it looks like to really be free.
The trauma that I found was like a maze
within the crevices of my soul
Taking them one by one I began to become whole
With every breathe I became more and more bold
I shared with others messages fresh and deep from my soul.

Today I took a (Loss) L!

Today I took a (loss) L!
I must admit I did not handle it very well
I did not go high but went so low that I created a tunnel
It's been a minute since I've been this disgruntled
I did not care how things looked or who was around
I had been pushed too far and was ready to throw down
Yes I cut the fool and was ready to risk it all
It all started from something so small
Today I had the chance to turn the other cheek
but that was not my choice
If you could have heard the sound of my voice
Someone came for me at the wrong time and
I was not going to compromise
I was not feeling the need to back down and apologize
Standing on principle or maintaining my grace did not work today
I let out everything that in anger I was finally able to say
I was ready to snatch a wig and risk it all for respect
My spirit was free and I didn't have not one regret
It was something I had been holding back for years
I got completely out of character and was crying real tears
I was not trying to be politically correct or do what's right
I was ready to catch a case and not back down from a fight
That old Shirley was gone and all I could see was black
I was about to throw hands and get people off my back

let
Love
LIVE
by Shirley Crews Taylor

I hadn't noticed the pressure building and the resentment
I was feeling
To my true self and all the disappointment I was reeling
I usually can keep my composure and manage emotions at all cost
But taking the high road —today, I took a loss.

Lord Help Me

Lord, please help me to get through this season

I am losing hope and I feel so heavy for some reason

Now, I have lived with the struggle to grow and regain

For the guilt of my decisions has caused me pain

I often struggle with the next step to take

I have to live with whatever choices I make

I feel so sad and I feel constantly overwhelmed

Sometimes I wish I just didn't give a damn

Then maybe I would know what it is like to just be free

Waiting to exhale, lord please help me

let
Love
LIVE
by Shirley Crews Taylor

Waiting On My Breakthrough

Sometimes things can happen to you in life and it can really break you down.
I mean, shake you to the core and turn your whole life around.
I was going through life like a paper in the wind.
I had no sense of direction looking back on it then
I had goals that deep down really I didn't believe,
I would pour energy into the things I wanted to achieve
I thought I had faith and I was always hopeful for a brighter day
But until you get to belief nothing will go your way
For a while there it seemed like I could not get out of the storm
I did not have an umbrella or nothing to shelter and keep me warm
You see sometimes in life your thinking can be limited and negativity can take a strong hold.
You can become very reactionary with your actions
and let everything into your soul
Until you can learn to stand on God's promises and
believe what he says about you
It will feel like you are carrying the weight
of the world in everything that you do
I'm so thankful I've learned the words
surrender, release, and renew

Because I've had to go through those steps at least a time or two
I have also been a bad lady just like Erykah Badu.
My mom would always tell me don't look like
what you've been through
There were days when I did not pull off the façade and times
I just did not care
Those were the days when I felt I had taken all of the bare.
I'm so glad I didn't stop or quit during the raw emotional pain and
that God gave me more days around the sun,
I've been able to find some deep belly laughs
and in this life have some fun
I want to motivate others to be kind and
make sure you love on you
Be encouraged as you hold on while waiting for your breakthrough.

A Healing

This smile comes after standing through such pain,

The harshness of life brought such strain...

The healing finally arrived

And it was only God that I was able to survive

Now I'm thriving and coming back even stronger

The clouds and tears are no longer!

Thank You

I had a chance to work with a man of vision.
The first time we met he had already come to a decision
for us to work together and build his plan.
I could tell right away that he was a brilliant and dynamic man.
He drew me an apple tree on the board to explain my role.
I would listen to his stories and in my mind's
eye see what would unfold.
He wanted a culture to train and develop employees and
his intentions were sincere.
I believed in every descriptive imaginary and vowed
to work to help them appear.
From the career page for the website or a customer value
proposition. I worked diligently and to all of this I gave my full
attention.
I was excited to work with him and looked forward
to our conversations whenever we could meet.
I was constantly learning and the projects
kept me sharp and on my feet!
I learned about culture and with his
thinking he was truly out of the box.
He was a mentor to others, humorous and as keen as a fox.
I had the chance to be strategic and devise a plan.
It was a pleasure to work for this man.
And being from Germany he took such pride.
His enthusiasm he could not hide.

let
Love
LIVE
by Shirley Crews Taylor

He offered me chocolate once and I took a bite.
I said "it's good", he said yes, it's German with delight.
I love the opportunity to work with you and
understand what we can achieve.
This whole experience is kind of hard to believe.
A manager as great as yourself is very hard to seem to find.
Thank you for your leadership and your being so kind.

He Will Roll All Your Burdens Away

Sometime life feels unbearable and you feel lost;

But there is hope in knowing that for us,

Christ already paid the cost.

His grace and mercy will sustain us and see us through;

Even when it feels like this burden is too great for you.

Take hope in knowing that you are not alone;

Our father is still on the throne;

Just keep the faith even when you don't know

what to do or say;

Believe and trust that pain will fade and

he will roll all your burdens away.

Scripture: Psalm 123:5 "Those who sow in tears will reap with songs of joy."

I Still Know My Name

There were times that I was so broken from this or that
I was buckling under the pressure and life had me flat on my back

So hard to believe that I made it through those dark times and I
truly cried a river
All of my issues that I thought I could not get past, God would
always deliver

My prayer life was not there and I would call
friends to listen and to share
They would take the time to hear me out each
time and always show care

I often felt bad because I know that I cannot get those hours of
complaining back and everything that I put out into the universe
For all the time I wasted worrying even though I knew it would
only make things worse

There were more than one sister that helped to see me through
When my prayer life wasn't where it needed to be and I just did
not know what to do

During those times when I was uncertain or
if I was actually going insane
My friend would always try to reassure me that things would
be ok because I still knew my name

Permission

I am giving myself permission to release and let it all go
To not feel guilt when I have to say no
Yes, I'm setting my own pace and not being afraid
to stop or turn around
To remember self love when facing
defeat and when life has me down
I am giving myself permission to keep going after I take a fall
I know my destiny is to not give up and to always stand tall
I am giving myself permission to roll with the punches
and know when to retreat
Though I struggle from day to day, just believe that
I will manage to land on my feet
I give myself permission to surrender
when the struggle becomes too great
To know despite set backs, for my dreams it's not too late
I give myself permission to laugh,
dance and keep moving no matter the length of the storm
To feel the pain, the grief, the depression,
but to not let the raw emotional pain be my norm
I give myself permission to not feel the need
to apologize when others do not agree
I'm so thankful to see another year and to let my spirit fly free
I give myself permission to experience
love and happiness even in a broken place
To find the energy to keep going when heartache
stares me in the face

Reflection Page
Chapter 2

_____

_____

_____

_____

_____

_____

_____

_____

_____

For The People I Love

I have been writing poetry since the third grade. My gift came as a surprise, but was a vessel for the shy girl to get her feelings out. I later discovered that I had high empathy for others and could literally feel others emotions and especially their pain. I often struggled with what to do with this gift of writing. I knew I did not want to bury my talents and gifts, and found myself reading and writing poetry for others. I would read at weddings and funerals. I have written so many "Celebrations of Life" messages for the people I have loved and lost. This chapter is for the people I love and my gratitude and love for them for sharing this journey with me however long the season. My father would always say that you have to give people their flowers while they are still alive. I hope the people in my life both living and dead could feel my love and appreciation for them. So chapter 3 are messages for "The People I Love."

That Final Day

When you have family and friends,
you do not always think about the end
So many thoughts cross your mind,
and you wonder if the scars can mend
You try to stay positive and focus
on the good times and not the sad
Finding the fond memories from the past that you've had
Most days that will get you by
You stay busy and not ask why
But in those quiet still moments, every now and then,
you feel that void and empty space
That no matter how long you live,
you know they can't be replaced.
So you try to move on and find purpose
on your journey in some way
Holding on to the hope that you will see them again one day.

My Dear Mom Mildred

When I find myself in those silent moments of reflection. I think about the people that I love and have lost. The memories rush in and the thoughts linger in the most unexpected ways. I think of the experiences, their physical presence and what I loved most about each person. My love does not fade and it feels even stronger as the years fade. The appreciation and gratitude fills my heart to all of those that were chosen to take this journey called life with me. The encouragement, the quiet whispers of grief still remains, but I am guided by the love that continues urging me to keep moving and not to lose hope.

Each year it is no easier. but I am learning to celebrate her life.
In honoring her, I discovered quiet truths hidden in my own reflection—the gentle patience with which she approached each new day, the courage that rested beneath her laughter, and the devotion that colored everything she touched. Even in the shadow of uncertainty, she taught me that grace could be found in persistence and dignity, that showing up for yourself was never selfish, but necessary. Her memory is a map of resilience, guiding me toward acceptance and reminding me that every facet of my being is worthy of compassion. The lessons she left are woven through every chapter of my story;

I carry them gently, as she once carried me.
Not focusing on the illness or the strife,
but when I think of my mom it is mainly

let **Love** LIVE
by Shirley Crews Taylor

her strength that comes to mind
A harder worker you will not find
She handled responsibility like a champ, but it also took its toll
Because of that she didn't live to get old
Lessons from her are now staring me in my face
You may have more than one mom to raise you,
but a real mother can never be replaced
I have to learn to take better care of myself,
and that it is not a badge of honor to work your fingers to the bone
Self care is so important,
and it is not a weakness to spend some time alone
You have to build yourself up and take time to self reflect
For your life, you have to start with your own strength and respect
I thank mom for doing what she had to
do with no regret or complaint
I cannot thank or celebrate her enough
for teaching me to show both love and restraint.
Sometimes a woman's strength can make you come across as hard,
but she taught me that being soft has its place
With her wisdom and reverence to God, she showed such grace.

"Big D"… DeArthur Crews, Sr. "Da"

There is so much that I could say about
my father that it's hard to start,
The first thing that stood out about him was his really big heart.
He never met a stranger and he had a personality larger than life.
He was a simple man not requiring much,
he loved his children—he loved his wife.
Even as a child he was a mischievous boy
that was always into this or that;
He was his mother's favorite—it was a well known fact.
He was different from his brothers in that
he was a large man and really tall,
He loved his siblings equally and for anyone he would give his all.
When it came to fatherhood, he ran his household with an iron fist,
I hated when he would spank me,
and then ask me to give him a hug and a kiss.
He was very strict with his children and did not spare the rod,
He wasn't always in the church but taught us to honor God.
He was even a father to so many that needed him to be there,
His house, his love, and his food with
others he was happy to share.
My father was a Barber and for years
he only charged $2 to cut his client's hair,
He would feed them invaluable knowledge

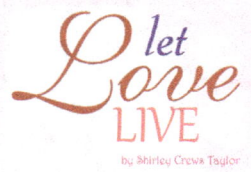

while they sat in his chair.
He had a great sense of humor and could talk trash with the best,
But when he gave his life to God, he put all nonsense to rest.
My father loved his church and to be a member he was very proud,
He could bring the congregation to tears
with his solos and really draw a crowd.
His favorite songs were "I Know I Been Changed"
and "It's Good To Be In Service One More Time,"
which we will sing today;
He taught us to give people their flowers while they yet lived
and he tried to show his love every day.
So it was only fitting to return to Brent, Alabama and James
Chapel for his home going and to be laid to
rest this Father's Day Weekend.
Thank you dad for your love and wisdom, you
were a wonderful son, brother, father, uncle,
husband and true friend.

LaWanda "Gayle" Rutledge

My sweet Gayle, you getting your wings
so soon came as such a shock,
but seeing you go, we would have never been prepared
Your loss will be forever a major void in the
hearts and life from all the love you shared
As a sister, Gayle was a prayer warrior
 that has been the source of strength
for the family since she was a girl and up till now
Although it is hard to imagine going on without you,
 we will make it somehow
We will miss your beaming smile that angelic voice
and how you poured into the spirits of everyone you knew
You were happy even as a child and kept everyone on their toes,
the family can't express the bond they had with you
You were never judgmental, you would always speak your truth
in love and for others, you would give your last
The bible says, "He who finds a wife finds a good thing and
obtains favor from the Lord
As a wife, she was committed until the end,
 even when time got hard
Gayle, as a mother was where you really saw her shine and she
was blessed with her son Marcellus speaks of their time together
and he says it was really just so much fun

let
Love
LIVE
by Shirley Crews Taylor

He shares that they often watched
her favorite show "Stranger Things"
and on how his mom would often sing.
Also that her favorite color was purple, she was "Just Chill",
and loved her family more than anything
We know you miss your parents, but is being so strong during
this time for his mom and dad,
Son, just know you were the biggest
achievement your parents ever had.
Gayle was very spiritual and even had a prophetic calling
through her dreams or prayer messages she would often share.
The last couple of years were challenging for her,
and losing her husband Markie was a heavy burden to bear.
She left us with the sweetest son anyone could have,
making sure that Marcellus was
a God fearing and well-mannered young man.
She can rest in peace knowing that we will
care and raise her child the best we can.
It takes a village to raise a child and
we will be with him every step of the way
For we know God will provide his every
need and we will shelter and love him every single day.
Rest easy my sister, we have hope
that you and JaMarcus will soon be together again
You were a beautiful big sister, mom, auntie, wife and friend.

let Love LIVE

by Shirley Crews Taylor

Our Markie

Both Jamarcus (Markie) and baby brother
Brian for my parents was a huge surprise
How Markie's heart and personality
would touch the lives of others, we didn't realize
He was the sweetest baby, such a happy child with the juiciest
cheeks and the largest grin Markie was
so loveable in every way that it's hard to begin
He was a clean little boy that didn't like
to be outside or get dirt on his feet
Like the whole family, he enjoyed his food and loved to eat
Markie was the fourth child of seven children and had extra
parents straight out the gate Being loved by
everyone and having a happy childhood was his fate
He and baby brother Brian were inseparable
and played together well
They did everything together, playing games like
"Dodge the Rock!", the stories I could tell
Markie was always a chubby guy but could
really dance and was very light on his feet
He would even bust a move and sing
when he had his favorite food to eat
Markie had lots of friends while in high school, then left to
attend Auburn University at Montgomery
where he earned a Bachelor's degree
He started working at Compass Bank and
became very serious with Gail his wife to be

let
Love
LIVE
by Shirley Crews Taylor

He became a father in 2006, and it really changed his life
His family was complete when he took Gail Rutledge as his wife
He loved his family and wanted only the best for them
Gail and Marcellus were a source of pride for him
Markie loved to dress in bright colors, bold stripes,
and he was comfortable in his own skin
He would often dress he and his son
in matching outfits, Marcellus was his twin
He loved to buy his wife nice outfits,
jewelry with the shoes to coordinate
He always tried to do romantic or special things
for her, and they continued to date
Markie really loved Gail's whole family just as much as his own
He enjoyed life, his house was always full,
and he was adventurous, often out and gone
Even though Markie had major health issues and was not well
He always kept a positive disposition and
if he had problems, you could not tell
He was a wonderful son, husband, father and friend
We can say that he gave his all until the very end
Though we will miss him, we will hold on to all
the love and joy he gave to everyone he met
His sweet loving presence and happy
laugher we will never forget
Our hearts are broken to see you go so soon and, in this way
But we know that you are now with our parents, and will see you
again one day.

GRANDMOTHER
(Mary Duff Crews)

I had a grandmother, I still wish that everyone could see;
I wish you could have met her, because she was everything to me.
She was my friend and she never let me down;
She was my hope, enriched with love, but now she's heaven bound.
I had a grandmother that would help anybody and anyone
not always being treated fair;
She was a brighter day for many who were in despair.
She was a mother to so many, even one for me;
Now, I am in this world without her—it's not like it used to be.
I miss her so much, but I try to understand;
I'm hurting right now, but I know it's all in God's plan.
She's better off I know, without the sickness and the pain.
She won't have to put up with the hassles and the strain…
That her life was beginning to show, for times were difficult
and the road was hard;
But no one can say that momma didn't do her part.
I remember times when I was so down and out;
How it would cheer me just to see my
80 year old grandmother up and about.
My way gets hard and my day seems so long;
Now that God has called momma home.
But I hope he remembers that I was left behind;
And without momma, my way isn't as easy to find.

let
Love
LIVE
by Shirley Crews Taylor

I can still remember her laugh, and her smile,
The memories take me on another mile.
But nothing will ever replace her presence, her loving
personality and what she was to all that shared her life;
She was a perfect lady, a devoted friend,
a wonderful mother and a loving wife.
It's still hard without her just living day by day;
But I know she's in good hands…
and the Lord will make a way.

Remembering (Dedication to my Loving Grandparents)

I remember when momma was here and daddy too!
If they could, it wasn't nothing for you that they wouldn't do.
They raised their kids, their kid's kids, and a few more;
It was like their house was an open door.
Daddy, he provided and protected his family,
while momma did rest,
For their kids, they did their best.
No parents will handle everything the same way;
They made their rules and policies from day to day.
No one is perfect, no woman or man,
But what God gives you-you do what you can.
Daddy worked on the railroad and there were many
days that he was gone,
Leaving momma and the kids all alone.
But momma handled things and did them great!
She made sure the bills were paid and that the children ate.
Daddy grew tired and left us here;
Momma had been tired, but left the next year.
Things around here just aren't the same;
It still saddens us to hear their name.

But we get stronger as time goes on;
Knowing we all have to leave before long.
The gave us the basics, and provided us
with a foundation from whence we came;
They created our roots and gave us a family name.
It's good to know where you came from and this will influence
where you might go;
I thank momma and daddy for giving us that,
because it is important to know.
I remember as a girl how momma and daddy would be;
They weren't' rich, or perfect, but they meant the world to me.

let
Love
LIVE
by Shirley Crews Taylor

Farewell for Now... Uncle Bobby

Bobby Lee Russell Sr. was born on August 15, 1937
to the parents of Nelson Russell and Melissa Lamb.
From the beginning, the world knew he was going
to be a real ham!
Although raised as an only child with his mom, a community of
relatives looked out for his care and made sure he ate.
Through his father, he had a stepsister named Rebertha Wade,
they didn't see each other often—but got along great.
He was born in Sumter County, Alabama and traveled to different
places to work in construction and even drove trucks.
He was a hardworking man, he became an excellent provider
and would really hustle to bring in the bucks.
He eventually found his way to Bibb County
where he met the love of his life,
On December 4, 1966, he took Jessie Dean Crews
whom he affectionately called "Jes" as his wife.
They started their lives together on Brent Hill,
then eventually moved to Westwood.
He was the best father, showing love to all 8 of the children
and for his family he did what he could.
As a father, growing up with him was very fun,
he was the world's greatest dad.
He loved to hear a good joke and loved telling them too,
what a great time we had.

let Love LIVE
by Shirley Crews Taylor

He was a kindhearted and friendly person,
you could count on him to do what he said he would.
With his family and friends, he was a man of honor
and respect, treating others as you should.
He was a friend to everyone, always had a smile.
He never complained about anything, that wasn't his style.
Back in the day he wore his linen suits and
was a snazzy dressing man,
His in-laws and everyone were crazy about him—
we were all his number one fan.
In the early 80's he had an Aneurysm
that left him paralyzed and fighting to survive.
Having to learn how to do everything again,
from walking, talking and feeding
himself--he was able to thrive.
He loved to listen to gospel music,
solving math problems, and hanging with friends and family too.
Don't get "Jab Slapped!", he would say,
and he just loved to joke around and talk trash with you.
With his children he was the "good cop" in the family,
the kind of dad that you wouldn't want to share,
He was a great man, husband, uncle, father
and grandfather that treated us all with such care.
We are appreciative for the 82 years we had him,
but our hearts are sad to see him go,
It will be difficult without his presence
and that positive spirit—yes Lord, we will miss him so.

let
Love
LIVE
by Shirley Crews Taylor

Thank you for touching the lives of others in such a special way,
We trust that God will give us strength to say farewell for now,
knowing we will see you again someday.

Mrs. Ella Ross

Wow! My friend your life was like a book,
you really lived a full life,

Ella (Mrs. Ross) was such a wonderful mother,
sister, friend and wife.

She traveled worldwide and brought the fun everywhere she went.

Joy radiated from her spirit, and the love she gave was heaven sent.

She had a great sense of humor,
and enjoyed time with those she called friends.

As a mother, she nurtured her children,
giving undying love and support until the end.

Even at work, people were blessed from
the kindness and joy she provided.

They just adored her, she was the only
one that many trusted and confided.

She gave so many the encouragement
needed to make it through the day.

Ella (Mrs. Ross) was positive until the end
and always had the right words to say.

let
Love
LIVE
by Shirley Crews Taylor

Even when she experienced sickness,
she never let it break her zeal, and fought a strong fight.

She was very loyal and full of spunk,
and was such a lady even when not always being treated right.

As a wife, she was virtuous and stayed faithful until the end.

With each challenge, she still spoke life and
we will miss you my friend.

We were blessed to be in her presence
and experience (Mrs. Ross), our Ella

The loss is tremendous for us all, it's no wonder why she is
Heaven's Best Seller!

My Greatest Test

With renewed hope, I held tightly to the legacy of strength that ran through my veins, determined to face whatever came next with an open heart. It was in this spirit of resilience that I stepped into a new chapter, uncertain of what the future might hold, but willing to greet it with faith and quiet courage. Life has a way of surprising us just when we think we've reached the end of ourselves, and it was in this humbling space that I discovered the possibility of joy again, waiting patiently in the wings.

When I first found out I was expecting, it was shocking to me,
For some reason, I just didn't believe it could be.
Then I got sick and they did an ultrasound,
I was glad to be on the table,
because I couldn't keep my feet on the ground.
To see a baby from the inside out,
It filled me with so much joy-- I wanted to shout!
I thought, what a miracle—how could this be done?
To create a child by having a little fun?
I got better and my doctor took me off bed rest,
I didn't know then, this would be my greatest test.
I walked around in constant disarray,
From the growth of my stomach and when
he started to move or play.
I didn't have morning sickness but I was always exhausted,
I was so unstable emotionally, I thought I had lost it.
I would cry and cry and cry,

76

let
Love
LIVE

by Shirley Crews Taylor

But this "mother thing" I would give a try.
Month's passed and I continued to grow,
There were so many things I did not know.
Then one night I had a dream that the baby
was born early, which came to be,
This was the most difficult thing that had ever faced me.
I can remember the day my water broke and they took me in,
Everything seemed in slow motion as
I thought back over it again.
I was in the hospital for ten days and thought I could go longer,
But it seemed that infection would be stronger.
I had to have the baby right away,
My husband called the pastor and they began to pray.
I was only six and one half (6 ½) months and
this wasn't supposed to be,
My dreams of a "normal" birth all left me.
They took me to the delivery room and told me to push,
Things would have been different,
if I could have had one wish…
For my son to be born on time and as a healthy boy,
But all my expectations, this would destroy.
I had him on a Sunday at 12:35,
He had everything and was alive.
I was shocked he was so tiny—weighing just over one pound,
I immediately felt I had let my baby down.
I was so sad, I didn't want to talk to even be seen,
I thought this was all one bad dream.
Then, the doctor came in and told us all that could happen,
even what he might not become,

let Love LIVE

by Shirley Crews Taylor

I tried hard to listen, but only heard some.
I remember they took me to see him later that night,
He was as transparent as a jellyfish, but was putting up a fight.
I fell in love with him at that moment,
this person I didn't even know,
From then on, the love continued to grow.
They told us he would have his good days
and he would have his bad,
I was on an emotional roller coaster—sometimes angry,
sometimes glad.
This was the hardest thing I have ever had to live through,
To have a child early that depended on you.
I felt so helpless even a shame,
I was responsible for him, so I'm to blame.
I felt so much guilt, even grief,
To hurt this deeply with no relief!
Postpartum depression was what I had,
I missed carrying my baby inside me and was always sad.
Sometimes, I couldn't hold my own baby,
which should be a crime,
But it got better and better with time.
"Gheori" (jo-ri) was the name we gave our first born,
I didn't realize how much he would be adorn.
He is a grown man now, that too is hard to believe.
It took me this long to write about it and start to relieve…
The frustration, disappointment, all the pain,
To look at the positives and realize my gain…
A beautiful son full of personality and joy,

let
Love
LIVE
by Shirley Crews Taylor

A blessing from the Lord—my baby boy!
The tears I cried before cannot begin to measure,
To have a child and the enormous pleasure.
Sometimes in life you have to go through some pain and you
won't be able to understand,
Why was a person like you dealt a bad hand?
But just keep the faith and continue to pray,
Because even through all the hardships, I wouldn't have it any
other way.

12:35

I still remember it like it was yesterday
I was at Woman's Hospital with my first child on the way
I had to come in because I was going into labor early with my son
It seems that my sac had ruptured at 26 weeks and the doctors were doing everything that could be done
I had to lay in bed with the head of the bed tilted down
There were all types of specialists around
The doctor said that I needed to hold on to him as long as I could
I thought that I could control it so I told the doctors that I would
They kept an eye on things and I tried to stay encouraged while laying there as I slept and ate
I was so emotional the entire pregnancy and would always cry
I was having contractions regularly but to give my sons life a chance to find strength I would give it a try
There were so many things I did not know while I lay in bed
Oh the things that ran through my head
I had my faithful family and friends that would come and visit me
My husband would come on weekends and
be as positive as he can be
Then the second week there I began to not feel well
What was happening with my body and the baby I could not tell
They had this monitor on my belly to hear my babies heart beat and it was my favorite song
His heart sounded loud and strong
But I began to feel bad and things took a
turn for the worse as can be

let
Love
LIVE

by Shirley Crews Taylor

They told my husband that if I did not deliver right away They would lose the baby and me
I my husband told me that we could always have another child and I needed to save my own life somehow
It was an outer body experience as I look back on it now
I told him I wanted my baby and that I can't deliver now because they said it was too soon and for our baby it would not be good
I was determined to hold on to my baby as long as I could
But fate was not on my side, my body had setup an infection and there was nothing they could do at all
So before I knew it everyone was
Running and rushing me down the hall
The doctor walked over and told me to push then I heard my baby cry so he was alive
It was Sunday, February 18th at 12:35
They took him and ran and I was not able to see him at first.
They took me back to the room and I was instantly better
My husband and I waited for updates together
That was almost 29 years ago and our son is now a man
Everything we went through had to be in God's plan
We saw miracles from out baby born at 28 weeks and only one pound all those years ago
I thought this ordeal would kill me but it gave me time to grow
Motherhood has been so rewarding even with
all the things I still don't know
My sons life is such a testimony and he has such a beautiful spirit despite everything that he has been through
It has taught me to find inspiration no matter what happens to you.

Everything You Need

Sydney was the name I gave you
I wanted you to have my same initials too
Having a daughter was such a gift to me
The choices for your life I hope to live to see
God has poured into you, turning into
a beautiful creation and I am in awe
So much personality and beauty you are
so wonderfully made… kisses mah!
My heart is filled with gratitude that
God chose me to bring you to earth
I am so proud of you already for what it is worth
Sometimes the things that come out
of your mouth leaves me in shock
Remember my baby, Jesus loves you and will be your rock
He gave you a brilliant thought process and you are so smart
But more than that, he gave you a caring heart
As your mother just know to
create your own path even though I planted the seed
Remember you are special,
equipped and have everything you need.

let
Love
LIVE
by Shirley Crews Taylor

Words For My Daughter

Sydney, you were more than I can have imagined
or even asked for,
From the day you were birthed, it was you that I adore
Now when I first found out I was expecting a girl,
there is something I must confess
I cried and I cried because my own self esteem
bought me much distress
I thought I would pass it on to you, so it forced me to do my own
work and start the healing process
I didn't want you to grow up insecure and like me, a hot mess
I wasn't sure of my purpose and I drifted like a paper in the wind
I faked it till I made it and it wasn't easy to pretend
But to my surprise with you, from day one that was not the case
You came here confident and commanding— you were a force to
be reckoned with and not taken lightly
I have watched in such delight and admired from afar quietly
I know that prayers were answered and I want to instill
everything that you need to succeed,
you will also pick up habits I didn't want to teach and for that my
heart does bleed
But I want you to be better than me, take what you have learned
and know that you are blessed and highly favored;
Go forward knowing you come from many strong women who
have fought and labored...

let
Love
LIVE
by Shirley Crews Taylor

For us to be here today, there were many names that poured love
and showed they care.
Women who poured into my life and all the wisdom,
I am bound to share
There will come a time when I will not be with you and
for your life you will have choices to make,
I want you to know that you can have the desires of your heart
and whichever direction you choose to take
As you mature, I want you to be aware
of your choices and mindset
That what you put into anything will
determine the outcome you get.
Remember to take pride whatever you put your name behind
Always know who you are and that if you seek you will find.
There might be times when you are you
might not feel sure of what to do or say
The great part is that you get to start fresh and try again each day
Life will have its crooks and turns
And the pain and heart ache that you will encounter,
oh how my hearts does yearn
But I know I have to let you go and share you with the world
I am so proud to have you as my beautiful little girl.
Remember with your spirit to take time to refresh and renew
Just know that you will find the answers, no one will know you
better than you.

by Shirley Crews Taylor

Cousin Ellen

When I first came to Huntsville, I had been told
I had a cousin that lived there;
While attending A&M, I was aware of your existence,
but I didn't know exactly where.
You and I shared a sweet Aunt Ethel
that I would always go to see;
She would tell me about you and would always remind me.
I think about three years went passed before
I decided to give you a call;
You invited me over and we laughed as
if there was no time lapse at all.
Your excellent cooking and warm heart affected me right away;
Then when I needed shelter, You invited me to your home to stay.
Before I met you, my life was fast paced-- working two jobs,
going to school full time and I was really stressed;
Then I moved in and you shared with me
what it meant to be truly blessed.
You made me feel at home by encouraging me to "be my best"
"not to settle", and "recognize I am special"-- You would gently
pound into my mind;
You were my angel giving support and
letting me know that there were still
sincere people who could be sweet and kind.
Even though you are very special to me,
There are many others who benefit from your generosity.
You introduced me to hot-water cornbread, and taught me to take

pride in my heritage;
You helped me overcome struggles,
 and over rough waters-- you were my bridge.
You made me feel apart of your home and allowed me
to forget my troubles for a little while;
You loved me as if I was your own child.
Sometimes we would laugh like schoolgirls in the dorm;
You were my shelter from the hardships and the storm.
You shared with me your world of joy
and what it meant to really be at peace;
You were there for me when
I found out my grandmother was deceased.
I only stayed with you for one year,
but made a friend for a lifetime;
When I need you…I know I can call any time.
A person with such character I am blessed to know;
I am enriched from your presence--you helped me to grow.
Now I take this opportunity to say thank you
cousin for all you shared;
It has meant so much to know someone cared.
I can't think of a more beautiful person in which to honor-- it is
indeed my pleasure;
Congratulations to a phenomenal woman that I admire and
deeply treasure.

let
Love
LIVE
by Shirley Crews Taylor

Granny

Granny was what we affectionately called her in the final years
She will be missed, leaving a tremendous void as
we hold back the tears
About her journey, there is such a wonderful story to tell
She completed her 93 years with grace, it was a life lived well
She was a proud, strong woman,
that gave so much to her family and community
She understood the commitment to service and for her people the
importance of unity
Granny was an educator and became the first black teacher
to integrate the school in her neighborhood
As a member of the Alpha Kappa Alpha Sorority (AKA), she
represented their mission,
and the 5 basic tenets of service to all …she clearly understood.
As a mother, with her children she was loving, but very strict
and wanted them to reach their full potential in life
She had a long marriage and really did shine as a wife
She poured into her students and the service to her community
was unwavering and impactful.
She had the ability to get you straight without ever raising her
voice, and was always tactful.
Although she did not think of herself as a great cook,
everyone enjoyed her food
Her meals were filled with love as well as patience and
dinner was always a happy mood.

In her later years, she loved to garden and
would spend time in the yard for hours
Her favorite plant was the Iris, and her yard
was filled with all types of flowers.
Thank you Granny for the contributions to your family and
community, you were a true pioneer
The love will linger always in our hearts, and your example of
strength and integrity will help us persevere.

by Shirley Crews Taylor

A Sister-In-Law

You are my confidant,
my shoulder to lean on --my friend;
You have shown your Christian light
when it seemed, my crises would never end.
You are my sister-in-law,
but we have grown to be closer than blood;
You have been there to listen when
I cried enough tears to cause a flood.
You never judge me and have even taught me
a few things or two;
Showing me how to use tact when dealing
with people and to be humble like you.
You love my brother unconditionally,
you are one he was fortunate to find;
You are an excellent mother to my nephews,
you do whatever it takes to make them mind.
We talk almost everyday about anything at all;
You are there to lift me up whenever I fall.
Even when I talk crazy and out of my head,
you always understand;
You have been there through illness
if nothing but to pray or hold my hand.
I am happy my brother has you in his life—
You have stuck by his side and you're a devoted wife.

let
Love
LIVE
by Shirley Crews Taylor

We all have our issues and storms
we will have to go through….
Thank you for being my friend, my sister-in-law,
and always there whenever I need you.

The Day Adam Decided to Let God Into His Heart

Adam joined church today because
he was touched and spirit led;
He made his decision based on something
his youngest son had said.
He had his eyes closed and Adam asked if he was asleep;
He said "no dad, I'm just praising the Lord
and God keeps closing my eyes", which was really deep;
He thought, if my four-year-old son
I can praise God, then what can I do…
His other son. was very happy for his dad too.
On April 22nd, 2001, Adam rededicated his life to Christ, he felt
inspired by the words of his baby boy;
Everyone in the church was filled with tears of joy;
His wife feels their life together will get a new start;
Because today was the day Adam decided to let God into his heart.

Momma

"Momma" was how I so affectionately addressed my
grandmother, Roberta Perry Heard,
She had a warm smile and a soft-spoken word.
Momma was the oldest daughter of 14 children,
she was a quiet leader,
She didn't brag or boast but was there for many who needed her.
She married at the tender age of 16 to the love of her life,
She was a wonderful mother and a darling wife.
Momma was elegant, with class and sophistication,
She always strived for the best and believed in education.
Years later she worked hard and even went back to school to get
her GED,
I remember her saying, "Shir-Ann, be neat,
save something for a rainy day"—
she tried to instill in me.
Momma could sew anything by sight better
than any top fashion designer,
She was beautiful inside and out- you couldn't
meet a person any finer.
She never left the house unless her hair and makeup was
together, which was quite surprising for a country girl,
Today she leaves her 6 children, and many grandchildren-- they
were her world.
Momma was very spiritual—she was the one that taught me the
Lord's Prayer,

Let Love LIVE
by Shirley Crews Taylor

To put your faith and hope in Jesus and leave your burdens there.
Like her mother, she was an entrepreneur,
running her own local store,
Though she told me many things, by watching her—I learned so
much more.
Now, that she's gone our hearts will be sad;
But we cherish the memories and the times we've had.
Even though in the latter years her health really began to decline,
We can take comfort in knowing she's now
at rest and has peace of mind.

My Sympathy

I knew from the very first day we met
You were a personality I wouldn't soon forget
You represent a woman that's very wise and strong
I pray you find the strength you need to move on
I know he was your life and the loss is great
There is a time and season for everything and
 your relationship was fate
I admire the business woman, mother and wife that you are
You two made a good team and your love will take you far
Just know that he is still with you in spirit and
the love will never die
It serves no one to keep asking ourselves why
Eventually, time will pass and you will regain your strength
again to fully live your life
Rest assured that he knew you did all you could for him—you
were a wonderful wife.
Just know that I am here for you as someone to share
You have my sympathies and someone to be there,
just know that I care.

My Blacksnow

The community leader, everybody's poet and our family man
The heart on his sleeve
He's so cool, it's hard to believe
He can sing, dance, but mainly spit—-
I tell y'all, Blacksnow is the shhh!
He encourages everybody by just trying
to live his dream and feel his pain,
There won't be another like him again
He's touched so many—even me
Telling us to get some black pride, it's free!

A Black Man

Brought out of Africa to work the land'
There's nothing like the strength of a black man.
He's the king of his household,
representing his family with pride.
He has a tough exterior but can be very soft on the inside.
Even if he didn't have a father at his house.
He can still be a great father and a wonderful spouse.

A Black Man…
You can find a black man that loves his mother
and will treat you right.
You also can find a black man that doesn't
love or respect himself and wants to fight.
He can work manual labor or hustle in the street.
He can be a professional, educated,
whatever it takes to make ends meet.

A Black Man…
He can come from the most deprived neighborhood.
Or be found in the suburbs,
wherever he comes from—it's all good.
When he is brought up to know where
he came from and the legacy of his history'
He will find pride in his heritage and whatever
he does, he will have the victory.

let
Love
LIVE
by Shirley Crews Taylor

A Black Man
Our black men sometimes fall into the traps
of the streets and go astray.
Leaving his seed to fend for themselves and
the single mothers to provide the way.
A black man lives a world where life is not easy and
there will be many struggles and much strife.
He may get harassed for his color, overlooked for a job or end up
in prison for life.
He can be very complex, deep and hard to understand.
But there's nothing quite as fascinating as a black man.

let Love LIVE
by Shirley Crews Taylor

We Go A Long Way Back

You were the middle child, so you were wild and free.
but I always felt there was too much hardship on me;
Maybe I was just looking at things the wrong way.
but I'm thankful for all the positive things you would say.
I remember when I was so heartbroken
the future was hard to see…
It wasn't until I could shed my hang ups that
I could start to be free.
One thing you always gave me was a reason to laugh.
even when I wasn't sure I was on the right path.
Remember when you, me and your sister wasn't
where we were supposed to be:
And your dad drove by and I thought he was going to kill me.
We were always good girls, and we didn't do any harm.
We just had to watch you when you put on the charm.
You had this knack of talking people into stuff;
Good thing you never got into anything too rough!
We shared a lot together, your wedding,
my wedding and Vals' too!
We each had a son first, and now you have
another child that's due.
Just wanted to let you know that I love you,
you've been a sister that's real;
And I wanted to let you know how I feel…
As the years continue to pass, I hope we will
always stay close and in contact;
Cause girl, me and you go a long way back!

MADEAR

You are a sweet person and a real inspiration to me;
It seems there is a "Madear" in every close family.

You love others unconditionally and try to treat them fair.
Ever since I've known you, you have always shown you care.

You were very encouraging many times when I was depressed
and during those times when George or Gheori were ill;

It's always so uplifting to me whenever you call
because I know that all your efforts are genuine and real.

I wanted to show my appreciation for all that you do;
I hope you like this poem that I wrote especially for you.

by Shirley Crews Taylor

Baby Jesus

*We can't believe this year has passed so quickly,
it seems the days just flew!
But God is good, he kept us and he kept you too.*

*So much has happened and there's so much to say,
I was blessed with a life and I know God made a way.*

*My son was healthy and went into the first grade.
My husband started graduate school and the bills were paid.*

*We thank him for wonderful friends and family like you,
We pray that in the coming years, God will continue to
bless and see us through.*

*We are glad that there was a baby Jesus and that he died for us all;
Let us remember him as we exchange gifts, however big or small.*

A Good Friend

Sometimes in life you meet someone
that have long-term effects on your life.
You have shared my good times,
and much of my strife.
I admire your humbleness, I know it will take you far;
You will be a blessing to others no matter where you are.
I have called on you so many times, often in tears;
I've shared my aspirations and even my fears.
Your advice has helped me make it through my day;
You always seem to know just what to say.
There were days when I was down,
I would look up and there you would be.
Whenever I need you, you always find the time for me;
I appreciate you and I think you are one of a kind;
You genuinely care about others and
when helping out, you really don't mind.
Thank you… my gratitude I just can't explain;
Having such a good friend helped to ease my pain.

Reflection Page
Chapter 3

_____

_____

_____

_____

_____

_____

_____

_____

_____

Beneath the Surface
Embracing Self Love

Embracing self and acceptance can be a challenge for many of us. Sometimes, with those gentle nudges to grow and transform, you find yourself exploring behind reasons for what you do and why you believe what you believe. Savoring peace and healing, you choose to do the work. I encourage you to reflect on your journey thus far and the resilience from heartbreaks, disappointments, generational curses and our choices. Standing on the promises of what God says about us, and opening our hearts to healing and purpose. You Got This!

Better Than Ever Before

I sit in my swing and feel the suns' heat on my skin
It brings sweet thoughts to mind and my mouth starts to grin
I take in the warmth and joy so exhilarating that I laugh out loud
I think of the year and I feel so proud
Some triumphs! I was able to push
through and I've had some wins
Great travels and good times with friends
I didn't give up when pushed against the wall
I matured as a woman and really stood tall
I let people know that I loved them
and will always have their back
I showed grace and mercy even cut myself some slack
I gave tight hugs and let the love linger from heart to heart
This year for me was a refreshing start
I was confident and I walked upright with
a smile and my frame was lean
I had opportunities to dress up I was fly and clean!
Being in my own skin fits me better than ever before
In the new year, I'm not knocking but kicking in the door!

let
Love
LIVE
by Shirley Crews Taylor

Finally A 10!

I always wanted to be a 10!
Each year I turn an age that I would never be again
I do not often say it out loud
about my age I was not proud
Since I turned 40, I created a theme to be younger
I have been the new 28 for awhile, but I can not deny my
chronological age any longer
In order to gain wisdom and in order to grow
I am writing this poem to let everybody know
I want to live, but I've decided not to get old
I will celebrate my life and live with all my soul
Externally, You may see a wrinkle or two and perhaps some grey
But inside my heart and spirit grows bigger every single day
Before I leave this body, I will use what
I've got whether fat or thin
Knowing that age is truly just a number and 55 when I add 5+5 ,
I'm finally a 10!

My Voice

I want to find the strength to continue to fight
Is anybody listening, and who really cares?
You better get yours, because you can bet they will get theirs
The pain is so raw and life feels so long
But I have to hold on and keep pushing to stay strong
Finding my voice again, it was somehow misplaced
I keep trying to run this race
What has me timid or stumbling through my speech
What is this inside I am trying so desperately to reach
People say keep it moving– keep it light
Even if the message is stalled from fright

let
Love
LIVE
by Shirley Crews Taylor

Who is She and What is She to You?

I am not proud of the fact that I wear my heart on my sleeve,
And how this often causes my spirit to grieve.
There was a lie that was told long again and even today,
it is hard to right the wrong.
It's in my psyche so deep because my mind
and heart has heard this for so long,
This myth is that no one loves me and that with others,
I am not really close.
It is always revealed that I am not the person they think of most.
Stories and memories from others make me feel like I am spying,
This keeps the myth going and I can't persuade
me that my mind is not lying.
I can see what others are doing and with whom
they spend their time with more…
I feel petty that it seems like I am counting,
and this hurts me to my core.
The myth feels like there is no one waiting for me
until I get there for the fun to begin.
Don't get me wrong, I know that there are a few to call me
friend.
It's just that when my phone is not ringing or
no knocks on my door,
This leaves me lonely and in life constantly seeking more.

let
Love
LIVE

by Shirley Crews Taylor

The lie is hard to shake no matter how I try
But I know there are some reasons why
A sense of community is what I need and desire so much.
To have that comfort of knowing that
I matter enough to keep in touch.
Whether it's a myth, I just want to know what is really true…
What will you say when asked,
"Who is she and what is she to you?"

I Am Her She Is Me

There is something different about me
It is not always what you get is what you see
I have so many facets of myself that I am still
learning and trying to understand
I am growing daily and stretching like a rubber band
Some days the flow is smooth and I just release and let it go
Then there are moments of constipation and
the release is labored and slow
At times I catch myself holding
my breath and afraid to take another step
Then I often feel like girl you really need some help
But when I return back to myself
I remember that I am her and she is me
For those days when depression is
lifted like a rainbow after a stormy day
I am so energized and nothing gets in my way
The best ideas come to me and I feel so free
I can look in the mirror and love what I see
But then I return back to myself and I am her and she is me
At times it feels like my life runs parallel with my other side
feels like the imposter not my true self and that this life is fake
Some days thoughts of another life seems
so real that it is hard to shake
But I am accepting each part remembering to show care to all
that I can be then I return to myself — I am her and she is me

by Shirley Crews Taylor

Fixed My Crown

I have been working on me which is a long-term assignment that
has included love and war
I am pulling from all of the resources that
I have gathered along the journey thus far
The struggle has been real and each day
has come with some type of lesson
Most days flew by and I was oblivious that
I was in another session
I look back at the decades, there were days that
I could not wait to end
I took my bumps and losses but vowed to try again
The idea of each day to have another chance
did not go over my head
A life of memories flashed before me and
I stand by every word I said
The nights that I could not sleep because my mind was filled
with worry and fret
Enjoying the special moments and facing the experiences
I wanted to forget
Thankful for the others that have joined me for the ride
I appreciate everyone that showed
me love and has been by my side
I am on a trajectory to keep moving forward and
to not let myself down
Finally my mindset is one of strength and today
I fixed my crown.

54

I cannot believe that I am 54 years old
But I still feel 25 in my soul
I thought by now I would have it all together
And my spirit would be as light as a feather
But I find myself have teenage issues and emotions,
problems with my skin
I know so many people, but only a handful that I can call friend
I just knew by now I would have gotten my sexy on
and that nobody could do it like me
I must admit I still do not always like the woman that I see

By The Water

What is it when I am by the water and
how the stress just rolls away
I know where to go when I am having an especially bad day
If the stress is high and the pressure builds
I only need to get to the water and
the negativity from my spirit spills...
I can come with all that has me feeling heavy and in fright
It empties all that shouldn't be there and makes me light
That moving water does something to me
It puts me back in balance and helps my spirit to stay free.

A New Year Begins

I struggle to find what next steps to take
Still trying to make moves without making a mistake
Time is flying and I can't keep up with the pace
I don't think I'm winning this race
My load feels heavy, but I won't release anything
still trying to carry it all
I tried asking for help and support but it made me feel small
So now I'm back to pretending with my half fake smile
Like all my outfits I've gone out of style
I'm on edge I'm on edge will I pull it off or choke
When it's time to speak there's a lump in my throat
Fear is setting in fear in setting in My spirit is broken and frayed
Even after all the prayers I prayed
I'm drifting I'm drifting and can't find others in which to connect
I'm isolating which has an adverse effect
I'm sinking I'm sinking deeper into the minutia in my head
I'd rather have a hug and be loved instead
I laugh deeply because I can't seem to cry
Some days to make an effort its hard to try
My life is passing me by my life is passing me by each day
Does anybody else feel the same way
My courage is leaving my courage is leaving
Is it just me that I'm really deceiving
Trying not to sin trying not to sin
Making the best of things as a new year begins.

My Food Affection

Why do I turn to food when I can't identify
what it is that I am feeling?
Am I angry, anxious, bored, excited or sad the thoughts
in my mind are reeling
I will grab snacks to put in my mouth usually something sweet
What is this unmet need I am trying to feed each time I eat?
Am I lonely, scared, jolly, or filled with happiness and riding high?
I know it is not just me, but when did this habit start and why?
I eat to celebrate and I eat to soothe my aching heart
Being a southern girl has even played a part
You have to feed people when they come to visit
Is it entertainment, my activity for the day, what is it?
Especially when I'm not hungry... I still enjoy eating day or night,
Now that I am aware I know that something is not right
I don't exercise enough to get skinny with what I eat
I can't even wait to the weekend to cheat
I will keep thinking about this I know without a doubt
Let me grab another snack until I figure it out 😍

In My Juice Chronicles

There were times in my journey that
I was lost and couldn't find my way back
I was bitter, negative and would not cut myself any slack
No one could put me down better than me
I became destructive and It took me years to see
I ate too much and drank more than my share
Those were days when it seemed there was no self care
I ate to ease the pain and I drank to dull it all
I was headed for one great fall
There was disappointments, loss and rejection
It was hard to feel love and affection
I was spiraling fast and my life was way off track
But with God's love and determination I fought my way back.
I starting working on why I was so miserable
and what I really needed
I put my drink down and to self-medicating I conceded
I started rebuilding my life daily one hour at a time sometimes
minute by minute
There was no turning back I started the healing process and
now I was on the mend
For better or worse I had to love me and find
the strength to be my own friend
To live a full life the way it was meant.
To forgive myself for the days of worry that I spent
Now with each day I find a reason to smile and show gratitude
Even when I have the blues I work hard to shift my mood.

A Little Me Time

Sitting here listening to beautiful music and I really start to vibe
My muscles relax and I start to come alive
Forgetting what I didn't do and what is left
I'm finally taking a minute just for myself
My head starts to bob and I feel the sensation in my feet and my heart starts to pound
I can feel my body leaving the ground
My mood is lifted and I feel a smile start to form
I remember life is good like when my days or sunny and warm
My burdens roll away if only for a little while
The joy floats in like Christmas Day for a little child
I bounce around and try to shake a tail feather
Now I feel that I can handle any weather
I'm grooving and bouncing and dancing around
Until that pain in my hip tells me to slow down
You can't tell me nothing, when I vibe to Beyonce
I imagine I'm on the mic with her and Jay
Until security hurdles me away
You know I love family and we go way back
But today just letting you know that I'm not sharing my snack
Well my me time is up until next time
When I take a few minutes to unwind.

let
Love
LIVE
by Shirley Crews Taylor

The New Birth

When I feel pretty, I think of those times
when I wondered if I was good enough,
if was sexy or had what it took
When I entered a room if anyone would even have a second look
Today, this new growth and self-love has really
developed into something deep
Appreciating every inch of myself standing almost 6 feet
Allowing myself to feel those things that I would suppress
Not always bringing it and feeling my best
Today my smile is full and bright
Finally learned to share my light
Sure of myself and whatever I face
Letting my fears and inhibitions fade without a trace
I guess it's sort of a new birth
Old things fall away as I live my best life on Earth.

Wake To Life

Some days I wake up to life, and I am not sure just
where I am going.
I feel anxious and unprepared to address what will come my way
and the not knowing.
I am doing this or that and most times, but I can find joy in those
days when things fall into place.
Other times, I long to discover the mysteries of life and be in
another head space.
I yearn for deeper connections, and have not realized that with
others I have really lost touch.
I finally know how it feels to live in a glass house and I do not
get out much.
I can see others passing with no visits,
but the loneliness will soon pass.
I often eat food when I feel fear and when in isolation, I find
comfort but it doesn't last.
Most days I often feel that I need a hug,
a kiss, and more time to be good to me
Again, the door to my heart is locked and I have lost the key,
ensuring my spirit will never be free.

You

You are special and I want you to know
You have value and whatever is required to grow
It doesn't matter what others say but what you believe
This goes out to all of us with our hearts on our sleeve
You have unique qualities that were given to only you
Use your gifts and treasure them too
You are going to make it no matter how it looks now
You will push through it all some how
You are a survivor and don't easily break
Don't let anyone make you feel that you are not great. (Even you)

by shirley Crews Taylor

I See You

I see you, and I know you see me
Out here struggling to just be ...
Relevant— in all that I do, in the lives of others even to you
Confident— in what I say and all my competence
Authentic — Real, with no facades or pretense
Bad — bad meaning good, taking life by the reigns
Accepted— for my accomplishments, my losses and my gains
Affection — feel love from others and give love in return
Educate— school others and deal with the lessons I have to learn.

Get Extra Help

The depression in my life had the real me hidden
like clouds on an overcast day with no sun at all
The negativity flowed from my head and heart like a water fall
My light couldn't shine the way it was meant
Just trying to get energy was how most days were spent
No deep belly laughs or smiles just because
Everything I attempted failed and I felt like a lost cause
I could not see what I had or find any value in me or even believe
When others complimented me, I still couldn't recognize it, and
positivity was hard to receive But today, I have my second wind
And a new life I begin
The smiles come easier, and there's a new stride in my step
So glad I did what I had to do to get extra help.

Sparkle of Love

Did you realize when we first met so many years ago—
We would spark a love that continues to grow?
It's not often you find the one person you were
meant to share the rest of your life;
I would like you to know how much
I love you and enjoy being your wife.
My wish is that our love continues to
grow and we build a bond that's strong…
Where we have a relationship that
can handle the storms of life
and whatever may go wrong.
May the happiness we've found be with us forever;
and we enjoy spending time together.

Awake

I am finally awake
Taken the steps I need to take
Got what I needed to heal
Now all 5 senses my body can feel
even my food tastes better and I am really living
My heart is open— I am receiving, sharing and giving
All of me I am showing up in every way
Facing all my fears every day
Continuing to do the work getting past depression and grief
My faith has helped my unbelief
I've cracked the surface into my future and forgave my past
This time I know my joy will last
Because it's not based on shallow visions, people in my life and
results of any situation
I am accepting responsibility for my life and any complication
I can laugh at myself and be the butt of any joke
Because I know who I am and how to "stay woke".

My Emancipation

Feeling just "Shirley", loving myself and it feels so free,
Taking things as they come, and I am really alright with me.
Whether a hair is out of place or I've picked up a pound,
To hear my own thoughts,
my inner voice—there's no greater sound.
Whether in yoga pants, rocking a suit or heck nothing at all.
I am enjoying life and getting back up stronger each time I fall.
I was a prisoner within my own mind.
My emancipation, I have been finally able to find.

The Smile Series

I am writing again and it feels so good!
This smile has been a long time coming and much anticipated...
Because of the emotional pain, I often hesitated
To open my heart and share my grin
To hold back on joy because I desperately needed a win.
To know that things would be okay no matter what I faced,
To let go of things that no longer served me
and the empty dreams I chased.
Today I want to go with the flow... love and release
No more holding back trying to keep the peace
It feels so good to finally exhale...
To end the chapter of a living hell.

So Thankful... (The Smile Series Continues)

So thankful just to be here to breathe and not feel labored.
I have learned to enjoy all the rain in my life because
they sometimes brought rainbows that I've savored.
To have loved and shown love and not been afraid.
Even if a broken heart was the price I paid.
To find joy where it comes and as often as I can.
To be a good citizen and the best and finest woman.
Thankful for the dreams so big it's hard to believe.
But to keep going, knowing the many things I can achieve.

That I must not give up even when I waiver and not feel strong.
My past has shown me that when I trust myself, I can't go wrong.
Thankful for the positive energy that
I share with others when we connect.
Reminding me to keep that self love and demanding my respect.
So Thankful...

by Shirley Crews Taylor

I Sit

I sit in my swing and feel the suns' heat on my skin
It brings sweet thoughts to mind and my mouth starts to grin
It brings such warmth and joy that I laugh out loud
I think of the year and I feel so proud
Some triumphs that I was able to push through I've had some
wins Great travels and good times with friends
I didn't give up when pushed against the wall
I matured as a woman and really stood tall
I let people know that I love them and will always have there
back I showed grace and mercy even cut myself some slack
I gave tight hugs and let the love linger from heart to heart
This year for me was a refreshing start
I was confident and I walked upright with a smile and a lean
I got dressed up this year. I was fly and clean! Being in my own
skin fits me better than ever before In the coming year, I'm not
knocking but kicking in the door!

What Happened, What Changed?

You ask about the new attitude and action
Well I finally said yes to my own satisfaction
I have been holding back for the longest time on me
Now I am going for what I want and taking chances you see
If it feels good I am doing it and yes that means eating the cake
My senses are so alive I am finally awake
Did not know how numb I had become inside
But I am finally ready to take this ride
There is a switch in my walk
People notice the difference when I talk
I am making moves and from now
on expressing myself in every way
No more keeping the peace and not saying what I want to say
To experience the journey more and
my whole life had been rearranged
Yes a brand new me, others will ask what happened what changed?

Blank Slate

I was born with a blank slate.
But it soon filled with limitations,
lies and things about me that I would hate;
I wanted so badly to conform and just fit in.
I too wanted to be successful, popular and thin.
My mindset was one of a victim and
I didn't recognize my own strength.
I could list what I didn't want or like at length.
When I entered the world of work,
I must admit that I did not have a clue.
I was lost, misguided and had no idea what
I was on this earth to do!
Faced with broken promises, lowered expectations, glass ceilings
and competition on every floor.
Deep inside an inner voice kept telling me,
"You should be doing more!"
Through my fears, I started searching for my purpose, my vision,
and my reason to live;
After years of soul searching, I discovered that I am encouraging
and a spiritual leader with so much to give.
I have put together each of my unique pieces and found my voice;
I now coach others to reach their dreams and to understand that
it's their choice.
I help others learn to grow and heal

by always speaking from my heart;
Your transition is not an accident,
but your opportunity for a fresh new start.
Believe and you can achieve….
Be encouraged!

Esteem for Self

When battling esteem issues, it can be a daily struggle,
lasting for years and as destructive as a drug addiction,
It like a heavy weight...You focus to hold your head high,
and get a handle on the situation
You paint on a smile and you can play if off for a while,
but eventually the lack of confidence starts to show
It creeps into all that you do, and you can keep
trying to hide it or choose to grow.
It comes a time that it is about survival and you realize like air,
you need a certain level of esteem to live,
Without it, your efforts are in vain —no matter what you give
You can self medicate or rely on others for love
Until you can leach no more on others and
true freedom is what you dream of
This is when things start to change and
doubting yourself, you can't go back
You put new habits into play, and things finally feel on track.
You can even relapse, there's an ebb and
flow to developing a healthy esteem
The battle can take years, and if you are not careful
it can crush your dream
So self love is like oxygen you might have to have it
administered until you get to 100% on your own
Don't be afraid to get the support you need until
that day you can stand alone.

by Shirley Crews Taylor

Journey To Our New Life

I am so happy that we are starting our journey to a new life:
Our relationship is a blessing and I am honored to be your wife.
Thank you for sharing your love with me, it fills me with such joy;
May God bless you with much grace,
abundance and even a baby boy!
I know you we both have had hurts and had
to go through some things;
But all things will be in the past and we will become new when
you put on those wedding rings.
It will be no longer "you and I" or even "them" now but "us";
Remember to always respect each other even when we fuss.
Love is not easy to find, but it's worth taking the chance;
We have to be committed, learning to trust
and there in no rule book in advance.
I know God is able and our future is bright;
Trust him for everything, and he will be our guiding light.

I Had to Take Off My Hat

I have been struggling with what to do about my hair
It has taken much thought and I have tried to handle it with care
You see I am in conflict about how to style
my hair and if I should show it at all
I am so thankful to have it and that I am not bald
You see the conflict invokes emotion and
about my hair I do not feel great
Questions that I ask almost daily…Should I dye it,
should I wear it curly or straight?
I try what they call the protective styles
The wigs and the braids keep my content for a while
But then I grow weary and feel that because
I cover my hair with something I keep on a shelf
That adding accessories to my head prevents
me from being my authentic true self
It becomes one more layer that I add to my weekly persona
I want to wear my natural hair, but can't get it to do what I wanna
I admit that I do not know what to do with it
Should I go to the salon and hours in a chair I sit?
Why do I over think this thing and when frustrated want to cut it
all off and start again?
And is cutting "my glory"really a sin?
I do not want to mistreat my hair and I want to care for it as I ought
Sometimes, for weeks I can get by without a consuming thought
(about hair) I feel judged and I even point fingers at myself and

by Shirley Crews Taylor

about my hair just what I should do
I know it's just not me, I hear others talking about this too
I feel self conscious and not professional
when I leave my natural hair down or pick it out
I can only imagine how deep in my psyche
that my reasons why are all about
So I wash it, condition it, tie it down and cover it with this or that
But today I felt unprepared when I had to take off my hat (Wig)

Alter Ego

What I admire about you…
First of all you believe in yourself so much, no one can convince
you that your beliefs are untrue
Your confidence is attractive to some and annoying to few
Regardless of what others think, it does not stop you.
Your smile is contagious, it's like a magnet for a good day
I love the way you speak your mind and do not pause when you
have something to say
Good, bad, or indifferent you are going to be yourself You will
not be stopped, by interference from anyone else.
In the cancel culture that we live in today, it's not cool to be
politically incorrect
But you stand on business about yours
and nothing has stopped you yet
Even when life gets hard you still stand
You do not bow down to any woman or man
An example for me as I love and continue to grow
No apologies …Thank you to my alter ego

by Shirley Crews Taylor

A Glimpse of Myself

As I sat on the side of my bed, pondering my day

I caught a glimpse of myself and felt a certain type of way

My legs crossed are so long with a beautiful Carmel brown tone My arms and shoulders so slinky and strong My stomach the one I spoke the worse about Holds my navel in the perfect spot staying in and not out My breasts, I never really would ever mention But they are still perky and my nipples stand at full attention As I sit on my bottom, I always thought that it was not much there But girls, I think my butts getting big— I swear! As I move to the mirror and get a glimpse of my face Everything is as it should be and in the perfect place My eyes are a dark brown and I no longer see the sadness My head protecting my brain and with some self love is healing from the mental madness My hair my hair… whatever the style or color…where do I start Appreciating my crown and my natural hair has been the best part My brows are thin and have a perfect curve without a tweezer Now I spot my large round nose, you cannot miss it either

A New Mindset & Data Dump

To shift my mindset, I need to remove items that no longer serve me and just do a data dump
I picked up certain things and my precious head I would continuously bump
see somewhere along the way I picked up values or messages about life and got some things twisted
But I am thankful that each day I am having another chance at it
See for years I didn't know that I was playing it small
Deep down in my goals and dreams I did not believe at all
I was busy playing it safe and was wrapped way too tight
I tried living a life without mistakes and thought
I had to do everything right
Even with the many hardships I wouldn't
take anything for my journey now
I have had some wins and losses but I have
to figure this thing out somehow
Now this paradigm shift this is not a snob story
I thank God for my healing and I give him all the glory
I am so grateful to love and appreciate all of the facets of me
I have learned all types of lessons and to be
careful what you allow into your spirit
Now I shake off negativity and can feel instantly when I get near
it I have to trust myself and to keep my heart clear

let
Love
LIVE

by Shirley Crews Taylor

I will replace any limiting messages and
self defeating thoughts that I hear
Connecting only with those who connect with me and
continuing to give love and encouragement as I lead with my heart
Pouring into myself and exploring new adventures
and be willing to make a new start
I will surrender and release daily any and
all things that do not mean me well
I am committed to walking with grace, finding the courage
to be vulnerable as my story I find a way to tell
I want my life to touch and inspire others especially our youth
Breaking generational curses, forgiving
myself constantly as I walk in my truth
How it started… a clean slate

Keep going … new chapters - sending love and encouragement

What Defines
A Life Lived Well

How can you sum up the totality of one's life and how would one
measure?
From birth to death—the ups the downs the joys the pleasure
I would like to ask this question and the answer to earnestly
know What makes a good life and what
 proof does one have to show?
Is it how you love and were loved and for how long?
What about the connections with others where the bond was
strong? Is it money in the bank or material things
that you can buy?
If so, how much do you have to acquire and tell me why?
What about the haters and the lessons you've had to learn?
To discover these answers oh how my heart does yearn.
You see I am right in the middle of this life and I am still trying
to figure things out
It has been a challenge to make the right
decisions and not live with doubt.
But each day that I wake I try to keep
moving and striving to be the best that I can be
Allow grace and love for myself and others
keeping my mind free

by Shirley Crews Taylor

I will continue to hug tight, love hard and
show others how much I care
To be generous with my time and always willing to share
For the girl with the wide grin and an extra dose of emotion —I
hope my time will be well spent
Even with the highs and lows —I hope others will say "she
understood the assignment"
From my heart and actions, I hope that others could tell
I will have to answer my own question
for what defines a life lived well.
What is your definition?

Reflection Page
Chapter 4

_____

_____

_____

_____

_____

_____

_____

_____

_____

When the Heart *Speaks*

This chapter is an eclectic mix of poems that as I put paper to pen, I was guided with words pouring from within my spirit. Words of encouragement for myself and others. Rhymes that include messages of healing, inspiration and often content that I was not able to read again once I got it out of my system. My writing process leads me to places and spaces of such emotion. On those days that I can fight against censoring myself, and I release and just let the heart speak...amazing things happen.

Saturday

Hello Saturday, I haven't done selfies for a while
I haven't felt pulled together and had many reasons to smile
I know I need to spread one on anyway
Just to be alive and to see another day
So hello Saturday, I did get out to play
Slowly but surely I am finding my way.
Met a friend, said a prayer
Let someone know that I really care.
Showing me that I have to find what
I'm searching for in my flavor of life and not to stop.
Yes, hello Saturday— I plan to dive deep and enjoy every drop!

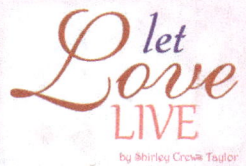

Go Get Em!

Remember everyday is your day

Just know it's your world and you are the man

If anybody can do it I know you can

So get out there and crush those goals, and don't dare quit

Just remember to me you will always be the shhh...

Go get em!

Encouragement

I just wanted you to know that you put a smile on my face
You have motivated me to take better care,
and take a few pounds off my waist
It's been a long time since I've felt this way that I forgot
I want to thank you for friendship, for me really means a lot
Should you need me just know, I'll be there no judgment
just someone to have a listening ear...
you really made my year and helped me get past fear...
Life is too short to not let people know
No one is around forever, sometimes you have to let them go...
but whatever happens you will be family,
and have a special place for me.
You opened my eyes and helped me to see.
Another side of life and opened my mind.
Thank you for encouragement and being so kind.

A Star Like You

You're bright, beautiful eyes see the world with happiness and
cheer; Your smile let's me know that you are sincere.
You are as special as your name and
your personality allows you to shine;
About your future, no worries,
whatever you decide will be fine.
I am so glad we had the opportunity to explore and share;
You should dream big dreams, and do whatever you dare.
Thank you for being such an inspiration
to others and especially one for me;
Keep your light spirit and let your heart be free!
Believe and create a vision for your life and
there will be nothing that you cannot do;
There is a big world out there, and it's not ready for a star like
you.

Today Was It

What if today was it
That this day was all that you get
How would you use this time what is the
first thing that comes to mind
Would you have more patience and even more kind
What about your things to do list, what would you do
If you knew this was the last day for you
Who would you want to spend your day with and
what would you say
Would the regrets overwhelm the rest of thought day
Would you laugh run and play
Those deep thoughts you have been pondering
would you find the courage to finally share
Would you make sure those you loved knew how much you care

365

Each of us get 365 days in each year
It is up to us how we use it while we are here
We can even break down the time to 24 hours in a day
Are you making the best use of your time and
touching the lives of others in some way
A few of us are lucky to have several times around the sun
Do you remember those times and was it fun
What does it mean when people say that was in the past?
Has the days faded like that flavor in your gum
Have you found success or do you feel like a bum
Are you reaching your goals
Are you touching souls
Do you wanna be here and are you content with where you are now
Do you struggle to get through each day
but you find a way somehow
How much of your time are you making
the most of while you still can
Who is still trying to be that best woman or man
How do you beat the clock and get your purpose
completed before your time runs out
Are you even sure what's this life is all about
Are you thankful to just be alive
What will you do with your 365?

My Representation

We all have a representative that ego allows others to see
This representative shows up in all the areas we are supposed to
be In relationships, we may have more than one representative
that appears depending on the case
We have worn these masks for a while and most of us no longer
recognize our own face
Sometimes it feels like the teenage years, where it seems
everyone is focused on you and the pressure feels great
God forbid that on this journey called life we make a mistake
Is your representation showing the real you in every way
When you receive a compliment, does their words reflect your
truth in what they say
My representative makes me look like I have it all together
That nothing gets to me so I can handle whatever
My representative has the canned answer to
how are you should anyone ask
"Oh I'm fine… I am ok and I somehow manage to say before
moving to the next task
You know I even have "professional" representation
that wears blue or gray to look the part
I clean up well and I use my suits to show myself smart
I also have the "just like you" representation when I want to fit in
I make sure I "dummy down" and
for each occasion I really pretend

Which reminds me of my "the imposter" representative
when I am reaching goals that I feel are beyond me
You know in the places you are not confident and free
Why do we have representation and when did it start
I know for me it was my struggle to speak from my heart
So I look forward to meeting your representative
that next time you come through
But, perhaps if I look close enough I will get a glimpse
of the real you

On My Layover

That storm has just passed and the waits over
It felt like a 1000 pounds was on my shoulder
The weather has turned to a beautiful day
I knew I would survive the flight and find my way
There was turbulence and a tight seat
Yep, I've landed again on my feet
Grabbing my bags, remembering to pack light
Knowing I will be soon taking the next flight
Recognizing the journey is about the ride before you get there
That I have options that can take me anywhere
I take a deep breath and purchase my ticket for the next trip,
the next one might be long
There have been cancellations already,
but I will try my best to stay strong
Not going to let the long line or anticipation break my spirit
No excuses, this time I don't want to hear it.
I hear my flight being called starting my next trip into whatever
Ending my layover to give in never.

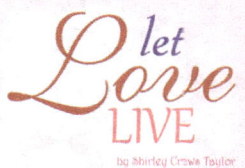
Change the Forecast

Sometimes you have to change your
forecast when there is a dark cloud
You have to find a change of scenery
when the noise in your head gets too loud
Some days get heavy and can carry on into the night
You know those times when nothing goes right
Although you try to stay strong and fight to hold on
Knowing that this too shall pass and not last for long
Even the strongest person can get weary
from the perils of the day to day
You pull out all of your survival tools and
even drop to your knees to pray
Even when negative thoughts creep up from the past
Just remember sometimes you have to change the forecast
Be encouraged… keep it moving.

It's Hard

Oh wow here I go again the pain is rushing in
and I'm dropping fast
What thought was it this time and how long will it last?
The tears flow and the joy is slowing creeping away
The mind can really run your day
It's hard when you feel unloved with
it really comes down to the matter
Sometimes you just get tired of all the mindless chatter.
What is it baby, what is the unmet need that you can't describe
Some days it's hard to get pass struggle and survive
Oh I could scream now! Man why does it keep coming to this?
If I died today, my presence would they even miss
I am replaceable and for many people I think it's already done
Man just when I thought my battle was won
Sometimes it's hard to take and these feelings are hard to shake
Am I anybody's number one, the main one in their heart where
the connections are real?
My heart is searching for something I can feel
It seems like everyone else but it could be me...
god let me break free!
It keeps coming down to me
Will loving myself ever be enough
I'm tired of the heavy stuff
My soul is getting weak
It's hard to stand on my feet.

Conversation With Myself

Hey girl, what you are feeling is perfectly
normal and no need for concern
You will have all types of emotions and life lessons to learn
Remember when you first got your
heart broken and you thought you wouldn't make it?
Or those times when the pressures of life seemed unbearable and
you thought you couldn't take it?
How about that time when your dreams got crushed
As hard as you tried to express what you felt,
your words turned to mush.
You have been through a lot
This is not the first time you got got
Remember when you were fired and had to sue?
You survived them trying to destroy you!
What about all those years when you didn't
love yourself or even like you?
I'm so glad you are past that now and you can love and laugh too...
So the next time you are having a day like today
Just pick yourself back up and be on your way.

My Mood

Today I feel frustrated and I am not quite sure why
I might be angry on the sly
I am changing my diet and trying to lose a few pounds
My spirit is feeling really down
I am lonely, tired and in need of attention
The type of attention I don't have the courage to mention
I smile and don't recognize the woman in the mirror
So often her souls is screaming but I can't hear her
She is needing something but not sure what it is or where
She often hopes to find what she needs when she gets there.
Where is there, she only hopes to figure out
It feels a million miles from here no doubt,
Maybe I'm just stuffy and feeling rude
But I need to find a way to shift my mood

let Love LIVE
by Shirley Crews Taylor

Get Out There Go!

Now I might sound insensitive pushing
you out there when you need a hug?
I am coming straight for you, and we won't
sweep this under a rug.

Time is ticking away, go for what you want today!
Hurry, who knows how much time is left,
If you miss out on your dreams you can only blame yourself.

Take this swift kick wrapped in love and kisses,
This could be one of your quick fixes.

This same advice I am taking for me too;
Your boat is sinking and the coast guard is not coming for you.

So for us, now is the time or nothing at all,
Take this knowledge and go have a ball.

Hey! I said hurry!
There is no time to fret and worry,

Go for yours and I will go for mine
Don't you know you have to put it all on the line!

For your peace and sanity there is no time to waste.
If it were not true I wouldn't be so hard on your case...move
forward to whatever you must face.

let
Love
LIVE

by Shirley Crews Taylor

Get out there—-Go!
I don't want to be the one to say I told you so...

Look! You think that I am playing with you, I will not say it again,
If you don't listen to anybody else, take it from your friend.

Cast your cares to the wind and take life by storm
Can't promise every day will be sunny and warm

Or that you will find shelter and stay dry,
But in the end you don't want to have regrets and ask why.

Get! Don't make haste to this knowledge that I drop...
The next thing coming is a pop...

Upside that long head
You must hear what is said!

Whew! I see I will have to tell you again and
I don't often like to repeat,
Words of wisdom, so get it while the getting is good,
Don't worry about doing as society says you should

Get out there and make your own path to what you create...
Please go before it's too late.

Man! Woman! How hard headed are you?
What else do you want me to do!

Stand on my head, put it on a bill board sign?
It's the only way to seek what you shall find...

this is serious and I won't be kind and sugar coat.
You have to save yourself——-rock the boat.

I am not going to let up because I care,
You have to get going if we're gonna get there.

I don't want you to be left in indecision and dread
It's ok to get off that hard bed...

That you have made for years but you can finally
take your blanket and go
Even if you are at your lowest of low.

Passion

Dream, pray, find your own way;
Stay focused during the day.
Imagine, live, take action;
It's the only way to get to your passion;
Feel; breathe, grow;
When the time comes you'll know.
Try, trust, believe,
Ask and you will receive.
Love, set goals; plan;
Recognize your strengths and be willing to take a stand;
Release, flow, give yourself some slack;
God is leading you and what you give you only get back!
Face fears, speak from your heart, and wish what you will;
Faith and hope conquers all still.

Take the Stress Away

Man oh man what a day
I am looking for something to take the stress away
I could start with a hot bath and a little epsom salt
To try to forget all the chaos created from my own thought
Where did the time go, it was but a blur
Sometimes I think about my efforts, and ask what is it all for
Today anxiety got the best of me letting fears set in
Woke me from my sleep and the random thoughts began
I tried reclaiming my power
To quieten my thoughts for just an hour
Before I knew it, frustration set in and the negativity grew
Nothing worked from all the tricks and tools I knew
I tried to distract myself with other things
to do with idle time to free my mind
But my abdomen tighten more and no peace I could find
I finally noticed that the sun had set and it was finally night
So I retired to bed to surrender my will until daylight.

Being Nice

What is it to be nice
Before you speak you always think twice
Why should it matter if people like you or not
Does it take away from anything that you've got
What do I tell my daughter when she wants
people to be nice and like her
Isn't that what the meaning of a good citizen is for
How do I teach her to stand up for herself and to be real
To respect others but express whatever she may feel
Even in love that it is her truth she has to communicate
I have to learn this life lesson myself before it's too late
There has to be a boundary or guideline
between being nice and kind
Why are you a "B" when we are direct and speak your mind

Being Nice

Battling Self Esteem

When battling esteem issues it can be a daily struggle,
lasting for years and as strong as a drug,
It's like a heavy weight...you focus on holding your head high
and not let your shoulders shrug.
You paint on a smile, and you can play if off for a while
But eventually the lack of confidence starts to show
You can keep trying to hide it or choose to grow.
It comes a time that it is about survival, and you realize like air,
you need a certain level of esteem to live,
Without it, your efforts are in vain —no matter what you give
You can self-medicate or rely on others for love
Until you can leach no more on others and
true freedom is what you dream of
This is when things start to change and
doubt yourself, you can't go back
You put new habits into play and things finally feel on track.
You can even relapse, there's an Ebb and
flow to developing a healthy esteem
The battle can take years and if you are
not careful it can crush your dream
Self-love is like oxygen that you administer
until you get to 100% on your own
Don't be afraid to get the support you need
until the day you can stand alone.

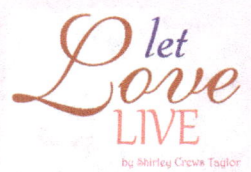

Set My Spirit Free

I feel so good that I could run a mile
And I can't stop looking at this big smile
Life had me on the ropes and yes they laughed
when I slipped and fell
Had me thinking my testimony and story was a sad one to tell
A conversation about lost, defeat and decline
It felt like no one would throw me a life line
I was taking blows and the punches that were below the belt
I can't describe the level of pain I felt
When you lose all confidence it's hard to walk
I experienced broken promises and nothing but talk
I discovered my strength in the midst of crisis and disappointment
Finally shifted my mindset and what I needed to be content.
Not to settle for mediocre and how to count on me
To remove the shackles and set my spirit free.

Man

Man it's been a while since I was quiet enough to
write something down
Life keeps me in a struggle and I have to go pound for pound
Some days I don't think I can make another round
You know how you can fall into routine of doing what you gotta
do Until your energy is gone and you start feeling blue
What do you do with the days of mundane
Hanging on to whispered prayers to just stay sane
Even as I document what seems to flow
The despair I must let go
I shift my playlist because I know that I am blessed
This moment will pass I just need to rest

Woman I See

I can not believe that I am really this old
But I still Feel 25 in my soul
I thought by now I would have it all together
And my spirit would be as light as a feather
I find myself with teenage emotions and the ups
and downs do not end
I know so many people but only a handful that I can call friend
I just knew by now I would have gotten my sexy on and that
nobody could do it like me
I must admit I still do not always like the woman that I see

Girl Girl Girrrl!

Girl! Get it together and dry your eyes
You have forgotten that you are the prize!
Forget that and release and let flow
No more stressing, just let it go
I have not seen you like this at your lowest low
But God has you and this will only help you grow
You do not have to get petty
Make your move when you are ready
Go down deep and find your place of strength and your fight
Sistas unite—Starting today let nobody dim your light
Forgive them, then forgive you and continue to heal
Your joy and peace no one can any longer steal
Take your power and be good to you
You know in your heart you did all you could do
Do not beat yourself down because you made
a choice that brought you hurt
Life has your attention now, nurture you and do the work
Know that you are a force in this world

Girl Girl Giiirl!

Reflection Page
Chapter 5

_____

_____

_____

_____

_____

_____

_____

_____

_____

_____

Echoes of Everyday Love

Echoes of everyday love includes poems about the day-to-day process of my journey. It is difficult to come out of the past and not jump to the future, but to stay in the present. *Life moves so quickly and it can be a challenge to enjoy the simple things in life, observing the small things in nature and just the*

twenty-four hours we get each day. I hope this chapter will remind you to take the moments to watch the leaves change colors, a bird singing, and the turtle to climb on a rock to get some sun or just the count of breaths as you walk and continue your journey. Take the time to get quiet so you can hear your thoughts, knowing that all of the answers are inside of you.

Fall

I love the change of season with the colors
of foliage and when the temps start to drop
Fall is my favorite time of year and for
a while the madness seems to stop
I think the heat does something to
my brain but in the Fall I am cool
I can manage my emotions better,
trying not to catch a case or act a fool
My heart is so full of love with a desire to do something
more for my people and humanity
I have to face the woman in the mirror because
I know it starts with me
My heart's desire to spend more time
with the babies and keep their futures bright
Sometimes these types of dreams keep me up at night
But just like the Fall season, I wait until it's my time to make a
move and not rush what I can't not control
Just do what I can to prepare until the reality of my dreams unfold

Walking

I started walking every day to help ease
my mind and tighten my frame
It's amazing when you live in the present things are not the same
I see the small things and can be one with nature just for a while
The beauty of it all always brings a smile
It's like tunnel vision and the things in the distance become clear
Your vision is brighter and oh the things you notice and can
hear... Like the turtle climbing on a rock to get some sun
Or that Seagull flying in for fish while I take my run (walking)
The oxygen fills the lungs and calms the thoughts
that bounce around in my psyche for free
I can remember my things to do and find solutions to questions,
the answers just come to me
I ponder everything but force myself to stay in the moment
somehow Just by walking I know that all is well for now

let
Love
LIVE

by Shirley Crews Taylor

A Piece of Rainbow

Sometimes the journey feels midstream and you have so far to go
You find yourself going against the current
and goals feel challenged and slow
The struggle is real and the days seem long
But you know that this too shall pass and you decide to stay
strong The weather changes so quickly from
clear to clouds and back to sunny
At times life is so heavy that it's just not funny
We have to hang on even when the storms come and go
During those seasons, I will settle for a piece of rainbow

let Love LIVE
by Shirley Caswa Taylor

Double Rainbow

But then a glimmer shines through, unexpected and bright—
A moment, a gesture, a spark in the night.
Maybe it's the echo of laughter after a long, hard day,|
Or the gentle reminder that peace can find its way.
You pause and remember you're more than the grind,
That love and resilience are treasures you're destined to find.
So you gather your courage, lift your gaze toward the sky,
Determined to press on, unwilling to let hope pass by.

Just Know

Sometimes the wind blows hard and
through the clouds it's hard to find your way
People try to be there for you but are
not sure of the perfect words to say
I understand the pressure can be so great
that it's hard to make it sometimes even minute by minute
As believers, we hold fast to our faith that despite it all that our
trials that God has not forsaken us during it
Though the tears may flow and all hope feels
lost and life is full of despair
Just know the father is still in control and
no matter how it looks, he's always there
Even when you can't find the words in prayer,
knowing your father already knows and will be your guide
Although we can't predict the outcome,
we know the Lord will provide
Be encouraged and know that you are
loved even when you lose strength
and the grief seems relentless
God is all knowing in matters especially
when it comes from an act so senseless
Sorry for your loss and there is nothing to say that will change
the situation and life has handed you such a blow
But God can in the middle and even in the worst of storms—
he can send a double rainbow

Something About Today

There is something about today
And it's like a breath of fresh air,
My mind is light without a worry or a care
My body even feels good not a single pain
It feels wonderful just to be sane
I look forward to the next challenge, in fact I seek them out
I am dreaming and believing again without any doubt
My faith is renewed and my spirit is strong
I am no longer just trying to get along
I go after what I want with precision and skill
Life no longer feels like climbing one long hill
I am dressing better and finding my swag
No longer feeling like a real drag
Singing out loud and have a new switch in my hip
Treasuring Love where I find it in any relationship.

by Shirley Crews Taylor

This Feeling

Sometimes there is this feeling that overtakes me
At times I feel it so strongly that there is some
other place I'm supposed to be
I really can't explain but it's just a deep feeling within
At times my day to day feels like pretend
I go to my closet and even my clothes don't seem to be my style
Most days, I can fill it up with business and chatter
But it's those quiet moments that nothing else I do seems to
matter Is it memories from a past life trying to come through?
Or something in my future that I'm supposed to walk into?
It's not that I'm unhappy or even depressed
I am grateful for I know that I am blessed
At times, I try to focus hard to discover what it could be,
But then I only frustrate myself
when all my efforts —I still cannot see
But perhaps it's right in front of me
I only hope that I know when I'm there
And that it's a place of love with positivity everywhere

What Awesome Looks Like

I saw what awesome looked like today and it blew my mind!
It was there all the time but hard for me to find
I have been searching for audacious goals and
missed the small things right in view
This is what overlooking simplicity in life can do to you
But today, yes today it was in plain view
I saw what awesome looked like for me and you
It was through my son and his message of strength
Until today didn't know what that meant
To keep going after everyone has counted you out.
Those times when your spirit was filled with doubt
But still I saw what awesome looked liked today
It opened my mind to stay strong and steady as I find my way
Before my expectations for life weren't real high
I was stuck in mediocrity and I cannot lie
Until today when I saw what awesome looked
like through the eyes of my son
After all of his personal challenges the battle he won.
What awesome looks like...

Wednesday

It is Wednesday morning and I am just starting
to stir from the night before.
I need to get moving because there is a lot to do for sure.
I need to bless others with my presence,
encourage a soul, help mend a heart,
There is so much to do that I cannot delay my start.
Flash someone a smile because it might be their only one for
today. Uplift and encourage someone to believe,
making sure I start with me,
Giving thanks and being an example for others to see.
It's Wednesday...

Get in the Game

I attended a two day workshop for the weekend
I left on the second day and I was in a tail spin
I was initially so exhilarated about the content
and the people I would meet
Not knowing that the second day would have me in doubt
and unstable on my feet I read, I saw and I listened with great
attention
The speakers spoke words that I could relate to and I would often
mention They spoke of mindset and reaching your goals
It caused me to look deep into my soul
The people there were open and seemed so different from me
It caused me to face some limiting beliefs that I did not want to
see That I am not living a full life and not content with what I
found
I am fearful, frustrated and it is bringing my spirits down.
I witnessed an example of what I "should be" pursuing
Right in front of my eyes, others were doing
what I "should be" doing
Until I can gain the courage to answer the call,
I will remain benched and my day to day will be the same
Father, please help me to step up to live in
my purpose and finally get in the game.

First Day Of Spring

It is the first day of Spring
And how my heart does sing!
Just to see another day and have a clear mind
Y'all that hasn't been easy to find.
I am so thankful for friends and the ability to write
The words come easily like love at first sight!
I try to be deep and think of something profound
But I let the soul flow even when I'm down.
The messages I write are for me to share
To show love and encouragement to others and
let them know people care.
I can be cool with my words and take a literally chance.
You know fellas, I can bring the romance.
But I'm trying to keep my mind right
So today I will keep it light
Since it's Spring and I am feeling the fever hit.
This year — I'm going with the flow and not pausing a bit.
It's Spring Time

Reflection Page
Chapter 6

_____

_____

_____

_____

_____

_____

_____

_____

_____

_____

Encouragement for the Journey

As I gather myself, the ups and downs of life… I am still in awe of how amazing the journey has been thus far. This chapter includes short stories and conversations about hope. I know that my purpose is to encourage the hearts of others. Now, I understand that I need to add myself to the mix. Making sure I love myself, and speak over my life. Over the years, I have been thankful for the words that come to me in rhymes and the messages that I am able to create to uplift and inspire others to not give up and to strive to be the best person they can be each day. Be encouraged and continue to hold onto hope and belief to overcome struggles and become resilient.

The Woman In The Park

I went to a park mid-morning after dropping off my son. I often say I will go close to nature and be creative so I had to talk myself into getting out of the car as I often have to do.

While sitting in the car this lady started walking toward the car. She appeared a bit unkept and was mumbling to herself. Then she stood right in front of my car and made eye contact with me. The tears started to roll down her face. Then she walked away. I wanted to go follow her and talk to her. I thought is she was someone's mom, was she married? Did she have children? Was she homeless?

Then she disappeared as quickly as she showed up. I had many reasons to not say anything to a stranger. I was taught to not talk to strangers, I was afraid she was mentally ill. I was afraid I was mentally ill.

Then she reminded me that that could be me or my friend or my child or my mom. I finally got out of the car and walked around the park. I found a beautiful bench by the water. I thought I would pull out my journal and write something amazing. I could not shake the woman that I made eye contact with and my heart was heavy. Well my heart is always heavy but the empathy was so great. I connected with this person somehow. I wondered most of the day. Of course it made me think about my life and how that could be if not for God's grace. It stayed with me because I felt as though I did not handle the connection correctly. How many of us second guess ourselves? Just me? The reason I felt that I handled the situation

correctly was because I did not help her. Why did I even think I was suppose to help the woman? Who am I? Mind your business Shirley! Messages that I have been taught since childhood. Where do you draw the line?

Then I thought about the freedom she must feel to live in the park and not have to be there somewhere at a certain time. The scary part is that it felt like freedom and I envied her somehow as I sat in the comforts of my nice car and drinking my coffee.

When did I become numbed out to society and the needs of others? When did I judge others that I did not know? Why is my picture of this experience playing out this way in my head?

It said more about me than her, why did I want to know her story so badly? Why was the feeling so strong that that could be me? Any of us could be a few steps away from financial ruin, and this wasn't lost on me.

The Woman In The Park

I decided to go to the park and be creative
during the start my day
I had just pulled up and found a parking spot
I wanted to get out quickly before it got too hot
As I tried talking myself into getting out of the car
It was hard to do but I pressed on since I had made it this far
So I took another sip of my coffee and listened to
YouTube a few minutes longer
The need not to take that walk was getting stronger.
Then a lady started to walk up that caught my eye
She came and stood right in front of my vehicle
and I wondered why?
Her clothes were wrinkled and she might
have been homeless but I couldn't tell
Do you need help, I wanted to yell
We made eye contact and she mumbled a few words as
 the tears from her eyes dropped slowly down her face
I wanted to speak or go greet her but was filled with fear
to ask for her name
Was she deranged…should I do a mental health check but she
was gone as quick as she came
What was in her heart or what was her story I will never know
Did she want to ask me for money but was afraid to say
Was she just lonely and wanted to communicate that day?
The fear on my face perhaps started to show
My need to help was halted for this woman

that was a stranger to me
Whoever she was and whatever she wanted was not meant to be
Then, I was guilty of the food in my hand, the logo on my car
and the many blessings that I cannot count
And suddenly I did not feel worthy of any amount
Should I have run after her and risk fear of rejection or harm?
Would it have freaked her out and caused alarm?
I was frozen and just did not know what to do?
What would you have done if this happened to you?
What could I have done anyway?
Could I even find the right words to say?
Next time, I will have more courage perhaps
to make a change for the lady in the park
A desire to be more open in my heart she created a spark
I connected with this woman because I could relate
I know that it is only grace and mercy that this is not our fate

It's Not A Big Deal

The emotions have been raging and out of control. Since losing my brother to Covid and really before that, I have to confess to being frustrated and out of balance. Sometimes we are out of balance and may not be aware of it. Since my brother passed, I have not been able to cry. You think the tears should flow with such grief. Then, I thought about my parents and how I didn't cry and this is the 7th year that we lost both of them in less than 2-month period.

Like so many people we just keep going, we've been taught to keep moving. For those of us called "strong" people it is what we are expected to do right? I have recently struggled with undiagnosed feelings. You know you can't tell if you are sad or angry? Those temporary emotions when you feel so happy that you think it's joy? During this pandemic and election year I've come to observe so many people feeling so strongly about different topics and things that they believed so vehemently. I've come to really respect those that know what they believe and stand firm on it. I realize that I've been wavering and exploring in what I say I believe. There is the saying "if you don't stand for something you'll fall for anything", Falling for anything can be a subtle action. I really admire those that have beliefs so strong that you're willing to fight for them and stand up for them. Even when others do not agree, they don't waiver.

Well, I have been personally experiencing all of that. I have had blow ups and deep belly laughs... not at the same time luckily. It wasn't until recently that I've talked to people on different occasions and each of them pointed out to me or happened to ask me

if I thought something was missing in my life. After some thought, I said yes! I was thinking about things like what I should've done in my 20s and what I should be doing right now. Then it came to me that I've been tired physically, emotionally and spiritually. Again, spiritual peace (not religion) is what has been lacking. I'm working on it, but when you haven't been renewing your mind and spirit regularly, it's so easy to operate on empty.

One day I was talking to a couple of people and the subject of anger came up. I had a good friend just start talking about how you know it's hard to cry when you're angry. It's hard to release your emotions. Sometimes anger can have you blocked. At the time I was not aware that I was still in that emotional space myself.

Then, I had a conversation with my son that was a real aha moment as well. My son has always been such an inspiration. Both of my children provide such profound lessons. My miracle baby boy, my 1 lbs. 13 oz. first child... Gheori Emeka.

My son has had many challenges in life but he's always had such a great happy temperament and light spirit. When I would share my concern about things,

He always says, "mom it's not a big deal." So, this latest situation that had me frustrated was I had some things in the garage that were in a bag that looked like trash. My son threw those items away being the helpful guy he is.

Once I discovered those items were no longer there. I asked him about it and he proceeded to say that it wasn't a big deal...just buy some more ...save your money and buy some more that's what I would do. Initially, I was very frustrated of course and it was a big deal to me! But his words were seared in my brain and I kept hearing it's not a big deal mom! I got to thinking why is everything

feeling like a big deal... Why was something new that got thrown away so upsetting to me? My upbringing did not include a lot of material things, so whenever I get material today, I really treasure it.

I had to acknowledge that they were just material things, and he had a point that it's not a big deal. This was a powerful lesson for me because I've been reading the serenity prayer for years, but it's been hard to apply to my life.

These days, I cannot tell the difference between what I can control and what I can't. Well, apparently there is nothing that I control and as soon as I recognized that things got lighter for me. I would like to thank my son for helping me to shift my mindset and like to thank my friend for helping me to realize that I am still dealing with some anger issues. I am trying to take all of this in stride and be nicer to myself. I want to encourage you to be nicer to yourself. This pandemic has really brought out a lot of thoughts in our quiet time that we may have pushed down. I encourage you to just keep listening and be nice to yourself and if something comes up that needs work then you find the courage to get the support to process these emotions in a healthy way. As you know every podcast, I use my gift of poetry to share . I wrote a poem that I hope you can feel on this one... let the healing begin!

It's Not A Big Deal

It's not a big deal mom! My son exclaimed,
He had said that to me before but this time wasn't the same
It lingered in my head and for the first time
I wondered if he was right
Could he be providing me with additional insight
I was frustrating myself time and time again over little
things that would get under my skin
I could feel myself getting more rigid and unwilling to bend
I had strong feelings about this I had strong feelings about that
I even get on social media and share my soapbox ready to attack
I noticed my emotions would ebb and flow from deep
belly laughs to fits of anger and rage
So many thoughts going through my mind and with others
I couldn't get on the same page
I thought my communication was clear but it has been hard to be
understood
And this makes me feel that I don't have a
sense of community like I should
Hearing a good friend say that anger can have you blocked where
you can't feel or even cry
Depression has such a strong hold on me and
I've often wondered why
Sometimes you think you have moved past thoughts or
experiences but then you find they are still there
It comes through in mixed communication
it can be very hard to get clear

I know for me it's been hard to push through the anger and the fear
I've struggled with feelings of frustration and that life
not being fair which has really hindered my mindset
My journey feels so long that I wonder how far I will get
I also recognize that others may
be experiencing the same emotions
and not recognize what you actually feel
You jump from calm to anger then to sad,
sometime it's hard to deal
So I have to thank my son for this powerful lesson that he put in
such a simple way
I am again reminded to be kinder to myself
and just take things day by day
And with this season of anger and fear,
my prayer is for healing for our souls
To not let our emotions hold us captive and
to release the joy and any negative strongholds

let *Love* LIVE
by Shirley Crews Taylor

What Do You Do - A Rhetorical Question

In July of 2020, we lost my knee baby brother, JaMarcus to Covid. It was an unbelievable loss for my family and so many others. He was 37 years old and had been on dialysis for 8 years. My mom was also on dialysis for 8 years prior to her death in 2014. The loss of JaMarcus was a real blow because he was such a wonderful brother and person. Our family was still reeling from the loss of both parents in less than 60 days of each other in 2014. Then, out of nowhere, Covid came along and stole our dear brother. There was no time to absorb the shock and the massive loss that our family and so many others were experiencing. My brother had been in discussions with a friend about how to get on the kidney donor list. She connected him with a writer that was doing research about disparities in people of color getting on the transplant list. In the midst of this, my brother was encouraged about the possibility of moving to Houston, Texas because he was told that he might be able to get better resources than there in Alabama. Before any of this could transpire, my brother contracted Covid. He had been so careful because he was told by his doctors that he was at high risk due to the fact that he was on dialysis. He even took a leave of absence from his retail job to be safe. He wore masks and had sanitizer all around. He tried to comply and do everything right and took all known precautions to keep he and his family safe. I can't say for sure how he came down with the virus. He was sick a few days before his wife asked one of our brothers to come and

help him get dressed and take him to the doctor. By the time he got to the hospital, he was already very ill. The doctors were not very encouraging. In the beginning, we were all very optimistic about him beating this virus. We had a cousin that was also in the hospital with the virus and was able to get stronger. They would speak on the phone to each other on the phone.

One day he called me very frustrated and was describing his symptoms to me. The struggle to breathe and that the doctors wanted him to lay on his stomach, but that was hard for him to do. He was becoming more and more upset. I tried to encourage him, but was very nervous about what he was sharing with me. He asked if I would speak on his behalf and make decisions regarding his health because his wife was not comfortable doing so. I agreed, and the doctors started to call me with updates about what treatments they would try with my brother. I had just gone through the same thing with both of my parents and a sister. But, as always there was nothing that I would not do for my family. The burnout was still affecting me from trying to advocate for both parents and those calls in the middle of the night requiring life or death decisions had taken its toll on me. Nonetheless, I agreed. For a short while, it looked like he would beat this virus. But his condition deteriorated quickly. He was in isolation and no one was able to visit him. I think next to death, that was the worst part of Covid. My brother had to go through this alone with no physical contact. Then, the doctors began to call more frequently, and the conversation became more bleak. They wanted to put him on a breathing machine to help with his breathing. It was the last time I heard my brother's voice. We did a conference call with his wife to discuss the pros and cons of going on this machine. The sound

of my brother's breathing on the call still traumatizes me to this day. His breathing sounded like a freight train and the whistle of the machine while he was trying to breathe was heartbreaking. We agreed that he would go on a respirator, then prayed and ended the call. Shortly thereafter, some days passed and the doctors stated that my brother was not going to make it. As his time to transition drew near, they called me in the middle of the night. I called my cousin to go get his wife and son so they could say goodbye. I had become the person that when people saw that it was my number calling, they thought it was bad news. For the past few years, for my family I had become the barrier of bad news. My cousin was able to take them to the hospital in Tuscaloosa, Alabama to say their goodbyes. He went into cardiac arrest hearing their voices and passed away.

I flew to Alabama from Houston, Texas the next day to be with his family. We were all devastated and in shock. As the oldest daughter and the "responsible" one, I was constantly dealing with crisis for others. It was a gift that became a curse for me eventually. But, I was able to be strong for everyone. My brother did not have life insurance for several reasons, but mainly due to his prior health condition of diabetes and kidney failure. So, I put together a GoFundMe account and my two other brothers and I paid for his funeral. Another celebration of life poem and service for my family. This time everyone was afraid to come to the funeral. At least he was able to have a funeral. The service was done outside because it was to be safer and visitors could maintain a safe distance. It was so sad how Covid invoked fear into everyone, but I was determined to support my brother and

make sure he was properly laid to rest. I wanted to make sure his family would be ok, since his wife did not work and his son was very young. Life became a blur, I came back to Texas with my family. I did not cry, I stayed strong and put on this brave front for my family. I only felt anger and disgust about his death. It was such a helpless and hopeless feeling like someone had broken into your home and taken your most prized possession. I managed to keep moving, but this anger grew stronger and his wife was encouraging me. The irony of it all was that she was trying to encourage me after all that she had lost. She was a very spiritual person and would share songs with me. I was thankful that my brother had found someone to share his life with before passing.

I was numb for several years after this, but I had to surrender and release because all of the grief was eating me alive. During this season, I wrote the poem, What Do You Do? A Rhetorical Question. It was a time where the climate was one of anger and disparities. I was very discouraged during this time and it was very difficult to move forward. The more I heard about my brother's options for a kidney transplant and that it could have given him a better chance of survival, proved to be too much for me. The magnitude of the loss became too great, and it felt like life was not fair. My brother was a great guy and we loved him so much. It still leaves such a void in my heart even today. I can say that I have still not found an answer that soothes my soul or would bring my brother back to us. But, I know I had to find a way to keep moving and release those feelings over time.

let
Love
LIVE
by Shirley Crews Taylor

What Do You Do?
A Rhetorical Question

What do you do with the anger, frustration and
weariness of all the injustice that has occurred?
Does it spread airborne like the virus or does it
scab over and dry up like a dream deferred
What about my brother and all of the people
who have been trained to trust authority and follow the rules
And time after time face wrong doing...
Is anybody else willing to walk a mile in our shoes
Why should we trust what the doctors say without
question or not challenge when someone says No
Why is it being difficult when you refuse to follow the status quo
 What do you do when someone shoots you for no reason but
hate Just how much more of this can we take
What do you do about the lack that seems too much to fill
And this is America, it just seems unreal
How do you pick yourself up and keep fighting until you can get
back to your corner after the bell rings
What do you do when all the need pulls heavy at your heart strings
How do you surrender it all because the cross has
become too great to bare
Do you regroup or retreat when no one seems to care
What do you do?

From Grief to Belief

I recently had the chance to see and experience a deeper love and go through the strongest emotions of pain, love and gratitude that I have not recognized until now.

I thought I knew the supernatural love of God, the love of a man and the love of my children. It took me losing my father, my mother and my aunt to experience so many powerful lessons to help me grow as a woman and spiritually.

This story comes on the hills of my having to deal with the loss through sickness and death. From what seemed to be despair but ended up actually being an awakening for me that has caused me to seek greater knowledge. I would like to share with you a poem about the women on my mother's side of the family, the Melton women.

let
Love
LIVE
by Shirley Crews Taylor

That Melton Pride...
I have it Inside

Things would happen to me and I would feel so weak;
I found that life was constantly knocking me off my feet!
My dad would always tell me to put on my coat of armor and put
my feelings in my shoes so no one could walk on them but me;
I didn't fully understand his advice and it took me years to see...
I found myself dealing with sickness and suffering
like no one else could;
I had the ability to go into situations and handle crisis
circumstances like no one else would;
That Melton Pride—I have it Inside...
My mother was a woman that I knew was very strong;
 she could handle her family and really hold her own;
Even in sickness, she never gave in;
She stayed feisty and strong until the end;
When it became difficult for her to walk she refused a wheel
chair, said she could make it with her cane;
Her independence and strength forced her to
push through her pain;
You would not hear her complain
even when her body was feeling the strain;
That Melton Pride—I have it inside...
She began to speak up for herself and with
the doctors she did not play!

199

let
Love
LIVE
by Shirley Crews Taylor

She carried herself with such grace until the last day!
I must admit it was hard for me
to go through and I was not equipped to deal;
I still have so many emotions so overwhelming that
I have to believe it was only God's will;
There is such a sense of hopelessness
and something out of my control;
This entire situation frustrated me to no end
and hurt me to my soul; When I was drowning and felt
I couldn't take anymore, I received a call;
It was my great aunt Daisey calling to check on mom and
give her sympathy for the recent loss of my dad;
Mom was not able to talk that day and feeling really bad;
She encouraged my spirit and eventually shared
with me that she too was not well;
From her enthusiasm and strength, how sick she was
I could not tell.
She began to call me regularly and she would even pray;
I enjoyed our conversation and she helped me
to get through the day;
That Melton Pride – I have it inside
I was the flower girl in Aunt Daisey's
wedding –she always saw something special in me;
She poured such love and was there in spirit
as much as she could be.
Once mom passed, we continued to keep in
touch and she asked me to come for a visit;
It was hard to schedule the time away,

but I was determined not to miss it;
When I arrived at her home she was so excited to
see me and was happy for me to stay;
She was very young at heart and we talked the first night away:
She was so physically weak, but didn't let it stop her from going
to church and teaching Sunday school the next morning —
Who knew by the end of this visit the powerful life lessons
I would be learning!
She used all the strength to teach this course
about love when she could barely walk;
She stood there and spoke with so much power
and I loved to hear her talk;
Before this visit, I must admit to feeling sorry for myself and just
off the hills of both parents death within 60 days apart;
I was ready to give up and struggled daily to try and move on
because life had truly broke my heart;
Then, it hit me that I had seen that same strength
and grace in my mom especially in her last days;
They resembled each other and their personality
was alike in so many ways;
That Melton Pride…I have it inside
I slapped myself on the hand and said "Shirley,
you got to do better!" You can't give up yet;
That was a profound experience that I will never forget.
Even when life has you down, you have to keep
going and do not stop even when you wanna give
up or give in—knowing that God will provide;
I now know that I can do this because of this
"Melton Pride— that I have it inside!

Character

As I move through the ebb and flow of loss and remembrance, I find myself standing at the intersection of memories and the challenges of today. The lessons passed down, stitched into the fabric of my upbringing, have quietly shaped how I handle life's sudden turns—those moments when clarity strikes, when the ordinary is interrupted by the unexpected. With gratitude for the foundation laid by those before me, I now navigate the jarring realities that demand my attention, whether it is a crisis on the road, a sharp word from a stranger, or the shock of seeing something for the first time. Each test pushes me to examine my heart, to reconcile the values instilled with the rawness of experience, and to strive for grace even as I confront the shadows that linger within.

Well, this has been a deep, honest thought process for me, and we constantly have to learn to forgive ourselves and others. It can be a challenge for each of us to know how to effectively deal with those out of character moments when they happen.

Character

Some things can get your attention instantly like
slamming on the breaks
when the person in front of you comes to a sudden stop,
Like having someone screaming at you out of the blue and it
makes your spirits drop
I recently had something happen to me and it shook me to the core
It made me question everything in life and what is it all this for?
I was forced to take a long hard look at
myself and what I say I believe.
I had looked myself in the face, and now my heart does grieve
I had to face the fact that I have been getting out of character and
did not notice or perhaps did not know
There was a darker side of bitterness, anger, frustration, and the
vengeance began to show
Ever since I published my book and vowed that
I would be my best self and just "Let Love Live!"
Since that day, life has often felt like climbing up
one long heel or a huge bitter pill.
I am tired of turning the other cheek or doing unto others
what they do to you, a few other scriptures that I could quote
These inner voices have taken me further from the authentic
spirit that I am. I had to take note.
Creating huge goals, trying to be the "Greatest of All Time"
(GOAT), and prove to my worth So afraid, that when it's time to
perform and shoot for the skies,
that I will choke and fall back to earth

Yes, character flaws like the fire of anger when I see the hatred and injustice for our race Self-righteousness, and indifference crept into my spirit so smoothly, it didn't leave a trace I had to look at the woman in the mirror and just be honest with me
It has been the hardest conversation that I had to hear, and it has forced to see
I realize that I must stop letting people, things and thoughts turn me away from my own ethics, morals, and values.
To continue to "Let Love Live" and be kind to myself as I have the courage to face any character issues.

by Shirley Crews Taylor

They Touched
A Place That Was Sore

By accident they touched a place that was sore
That hurt that no one knew about that you thought
wasn't there anymore?
You get up daily going through your day and get dressed,
When others ask how you are you say child, I'm blessed
You are just doing you... you smile, laugh and even play
It is not until a word is spoken that you didn't expect them to
say... Then a pain hits you so hard and the feelings are so raw
What you thought was gone or healed was just numb and now
begins to thaw
Who told you words don't hurt and just shake it off and move on?
How have you packed your feelings down to be strong?
Was it the donut or a honey bun?
Did you go shopping, party, or have sex to have some fun?
Do you grab the alcohol or your drug of choice?
Was your sore spot due to mommy or daddy withholding their
love or the word "divorce"?
Did you use distraction, sadness or anger to cover your pain or
your sore spot?
Were you in deep denial about how you felt, that you didn't
recognize what was real so you got got?
It's like going to get a massage and they touch all the
places that you didn't know were tender.

Let Love LIVE
by Shirley Crews Taylor

You try to breathe though it... just surrender.
Well that is what can happen as you go through
your journey and not pay any mind,
To the left-over hurts from years ago like a bomb
in a land mine for others to accidentally find
Was it your 6th grade teacher that said you'd
never amount to anything?
Was it your guy that treated you like you weren't worthy of a ring?
Or someone said something, and you just weren't ready?
That the words left you feeling emotionally fragile and unsteady?
It could have been your own words that cut so deep,
Because during those quiet times when
no one is around feelings start to creep.
Next time you get touched where you are sore,
now that you know what move you will make?
Will you search deeper for answers and seek to face your pain
because you've taken all you can take?
Or will you maintain the status quo using your energy
to not let anybody see and just let it go?

When Responsibility Became A Bad Word

Responsibility is really choking me
I want so desperately to be free
some days I dream of escaping to Canada or Mexico
when the pressure is really high that's when I most want to go
It started with being the oldest child to parents
who were not yet mature
I questioned why things were the way they were but in the end, I
still wasn't sure
I was trying to be a good girl doing what I was told
that I needed to stay humble and not be bold
not to talk back or ever asked why to settle down
with a really nice guy remember big girls don't cry
I brought responsibility from childhood to adult life now
But for me responsibility has become a bad word somehow
Responsibility is really choking me
I want so desperately to be free
some days I dream of escaping to Canada or Mexico
when the pressure is really high that's when I most want to go
It started with being the oldest child to parents
who were not yet mature
I questioned things but in the end, I still wasn't sure why
I was trying to be a good girl doing what I was told
that I needed to stay humble and not be bold

I would question these ideals and other things and
even now I am still do not know
I was never a child and had to take care of everything and
everyone and no strain I should show
I was taught to not to talk back or ever ask why
To settle down with a really nice guy and remember
big girls don't cry
I brought responsibility from childhood to adult life now
But for me responsibility has become a bad word somehow

My Cup Has A Leak

I have started sharing messages in 2020 and I always want to encourage the hearts of others. We are living in uncertainty and fears and anxiety are high. I have been listening to Sam Cooke and somebody eases my troubling mind. I am an ole soul and enjoy his music and how you can feel what he is trying to tell you. I hope you feel me in my writing.

I'm sure we all need to have our minds eased right now. Tonight, I want to talk about filling our spirits and what this looks like when something is missing or our minds are troubled.

How many of us are helpers…givers… we live to be there for others. This podcast, like others, will end with a poem that I wrote. This poem is entitled My cup has a leak. No not a literal cup but my spiritual cup. I have been guilty of not being able to replenish my spirit on a daily basis and my energy and mindset is limited.

Do we know what fills our cup? Are we willing to do the work to find out? Well, for me I have found that it is a matter of survival. I can't keep going with my cup having a leak. Let's work together to find out what fills our cup and how we can fix any leaks. Thanks for listening… My cup has a leak.

My Cup Has A Leak

I think my cup must have a leak because it is always low
I try to stay on top of it but it tends to show
Each time I have a challenge, it makes me and want to retreat
Or dealing with the day-to-day to keep all the balls in the air,
knocks me to my feet

My cup has a leak

My cup is empty often and is in need of a constant refill
The more I intake, Nothing seems to answer this thirst that I feel
When its time to be there for others, im Johnny on the spot
I give and I give until it is all that I've got

My cup has a leak

Even when I think it is full or that
I am getting with I need to survive
I still struggle to maintain and gain
the momentum to thrive
Times are uncertain and the challenge is real I need to get a repair
It is hard to cope and not end up in despair
Be encouraged and let me know if your spiritual
cup has a leak and how you will work on it.

let
Love
LIVE
by Shirley Crews Taylor

A Time of Crisis

I received a call from home informing me that my brother Bruce has suddenly become ill. My mom had just started back working from an extended layoff. She could not afford to take off, so at a moment's notice, I decided to drop everything to come and help out. I scheduled a flight the next day to Alabama. I cannot remember any of the flight except it was quick and I was landing safely.

As I left Birmingham's International airport, I was greeted with a breathtaking view of bright city lights and a beautiful skyline. I knew once I rented a car and left the city on the interstate, the view would change drastically. It's amazing to me that in Alabama, the interstate highways are better.

The roads are really nice—smooth! As a little girl growing up here, I didn't realize how nice the interstate highway was until I moved to Houston, Texas. Driving down Interstate 20/59, to the hospital in Tuscaloosa, I noticed the beautiful greenery of trees, and how the hills seemed to flow across the land. The scenery was very nice, postcard perfect from the highway.

Once I made it to the hospital, it was after 9p.m. I was relieved to find that visitors were allowed inside that late, but yet it was a bit disturbing for security reasons. I was given directions, and I headed to my brother's room. As I entered the room, there were cards around expressing encouraging "get well" sediments and one "It's A Girl! Balloon from a cheap, comedic cousin.

I found my brother laying there with prongs in his nose to supply him with oxygen. From the expression in his eyes, he was very

happy to see me. He also had this sad "puppy dog" expression and at that moment, I finally understood why my mom had always tried to protect him-- she sensed his vulnerabilities. His voice was extremely hoarse. He had gained a tremendous amount of weight since I last saw him. His appearance was of an unshaven man with a pale face. His arms were red and swollen from the many IV sticks and collapsed veins. There was a large tube sticking out of his side draining infected fluid from his chest cavity down into a container that held a foul smelling, brownish-green substance.

I took a moment to briefly update myself on his condition. He explained that he had developed Pneumonia and a large abscess in his right lung. His prognosis for survival was only 40%. He almost waited too long to get treatment and would need to be carefully monitored. The doctor came in early the next morning to check on him. He explained that my brother would have a long way to go if he was to beat this serious infection. His prognoses sounded bleak and that recovery could be weeks, even months away. I posed questions to get details and clarification. It was a pleasant surprise to find a doctor that appeared very knowledgeable and genuinely concerned. He was very thorough in his explanation and I understood the seriousness of my brother's condition. Given my Alabama history and previous experiences as a black citizen, I expected to be met with arrogance and ignorance, but was instead greeted with empathy and respect. I must admit my expectations were not to find pleasant, cooperative people, but unlike past experiences I found friendly, helpful people throughout my stay with my brother. My brother was fragile and understandably fearful that he might not make it. For the first time I thought about my brother's mortality. I wondered, "what was his relationship

with God?" Whatever his relationship, I was concerned for him. Seeing him in this condition brought back a stream of memories. Bruce and I had always had a turbulent relationship—to put it mildly, we hated each other. We used to fight all the time, even in college. But here I was flying across three states to get near him. Watching him interact with the nurses and doctors most times barely able to speak, showed a vulnerability about him that appeared visibly above the surface. It had always been just below the surface and was massed with arrogance and had not been clear to the naked eye. I really felt for my brother. I realized his plight. He was afraid…he was alone…he was very ill. Later that morning my dad came up for a visit. He walked in wearing his blue and white fishing cap and a big smile. My dad has one of the brightest smiles I have ever seen. It always made me feel better to see him smile. But today, I could see the worry and fear in his eyes. He was very concerned about Bruce. My dad hides his worries behind his bright smile. We were able to converse and entertain each other while the nurses cared for Bruce. That afternoon my mom came in with my two younger brothers, JaMarcus and Brian. They had really grown and the youngest was taller than I was now. My mom walked in last. She was very relieved to see me. I looked long and hard at my mom. She was a very beautiful

50-year-old woman that was starting to age from years of worry, hardships, and poverty. The wrinkles on her face reflected the hard knocks of life. She had changed out of her work clothes into this cute sundress and sandals. After an eight-hour day of standing on her feet to assemble toys in a tin warehouse, she was filled with concerns over Bruce. Our family was pulling together to share our concern and support for him. This was an official family

crisis. My family consists of 5 children, four boys and a girl. I was the oldest and the only girl. My two older brothers were a year apart from me and I'm sixteen years older than my two younger brothers are. We later acquired two sisters when my parents took in two younger cousins after my grandmother died. We have an extended family with many cousins that are like sisters and brothers. We had a small reunion in his hospital room trying to be strong for each other. Bruce was encouraged by all the support from the community. The pastor would come by to pray with him and the neighbors sent best wishes daily. I think this was the first time that Bruce was able to see how many people genuinely cared about him. We all suffered with low self-esteem growing up and didn't always recognize how special we each were. Every night we would congregate in Bruce's room to discuss his condition and show our support. Then my parents and younger brothers would return home 30 miles away for work and school the next day.

I stayed at the hospital with Bruce. He would have his greatest struggles each night after 9p.m. He would have difficulty breathing and the pain medication would wear off before it was time to administer more. I did what I could do to comfort him. Fluffing his pillow so he would be comfortable having tubes in his side and by now, his back. He liked his pillow a certain way and I had developed the perfect formula to keep him comfortable. Seeing him in this condition really broke my heart. He was really struggling to survive and was in great pain regularly. He was under the constant threat of having to have surgery to remove the abscess because it was not dissolving. This surgery would mean he would not be able to do the same work as before. I would wipe the tears from his eyes and tell him to be strong, to believe and keep the

faith. Just being with him through the night, I think helped him hold on until morning. Each night went by with very few hours of sleep, but was full of excitement.

One night my brother had been given stronger medication and was completely out of it. I thought illegal drugs had power, but the pharmacy had the "good stuff" that night. It was almost comical the way his nurses tried to inspect his condition. They asked him his name and his response was not appropriate.. They asked him if he knew me. He looked over at me with an expression of a drunken guy out at a club who had just gotten up the courage to come ask a lady to dance. He did get to rest that night! Near the end of the week, he was visibly better. His voice was stronger and he had more stamina. The antibiotics seemed to be working and it appeared he had eluded surgery.

The weekend was approaching and soon I would have to return to my family in Houston. I felt better returning home knowing he was doing much better and feeling that he would be okay. I felt comfortable leaving him since by this time, our brother Adam had driven from Texas to be with him. I felt confident to leave that Saturday going to my hometown to stay over with my parents and catch a flight out the next afternoon. I wished him well and started to drive home with my mom and younger brothers. It had been an exhausting five nights and I looked forward to getting a good night's rest.

As I got closer to my hometown of Brent, the view changed. There was still greenery and hills, but there wasn't a skyline of bright city lights. The rural town was smaller, and the neighborhood looked deserted. The only major difference from a deserted town and my neighborhood was that there were still people stirring. Generation

after generation of families can be found walking the streets, sitting on porches, somehow creating an existence for themselves. There is no visible growth, just deterioration. Most of the houses have years of no repair or no major upkeep. The town does have more restaurants, even a McDonalds—A symbol of the American dream. When I arrived at my parent's home of 35 years, this time I seemed more aware of the small things that I hadn't noticed before. I must have stopped hundreds of times over the past 15 years since I left home. I hadn't realized that the pictures on the walls have been in the same place for more than 20 years. Everything has remained the same. Looking with the naked eye, my parents appeared to not have progressed economically at all. It was commendable by most standards to even own a home or even make ends meet. I admire what my parents were able to accomplish with minimum wage jobs. When I was in the ninth grade, my dad stopped working because of a back injury. He has always been a very large man standing 6'3" tall and weighing over 350 pounds. In the early years my dad had been employed by a lumberyard doing the work of two men lifting heavy logs and placing them onto a machine to trim the bark. This manual labor position took its toll over the years. My mom worked for a toy factory as an Assembly worker. The factory would remain open for 6 to 9 months, and then she would draw unemployment benefits for the rest of the year. For 10 years my dad waited patiently on his disability benefits. I especially admired my dad for his faith. For years he would tell stories to anyone who would listen about what he would do when.

He got his money! His disability from social security claim finally was approved. I used to secretly feel sorry for him, because I didn't share his beliefs of ever getting any disability benefits.

During those times when my mom was about to crack from frustration and exhaustion of responsibilities, she would be very cruel about my dad's dreams of disability benefits. My dad reminded me of the story of Job from the bible. It seemed dad might have fared better if he had given up his faith and cursed God. His wife and kids were losing respect for him, his friends deserted him, and bill collectors hunted him down like a convict wanted by the FBI. Although there were times when his light deemed, it never went out. In February 1991, days after his mother had passed, he received a ten thousand-dollar check in the mail for owed disability benefits. My parents are a perfect example of perseverance and of people that made the best of life from the cards they were dealt. Sitting in my parents living room made me conscious of how much I have grown. I have relocated close to 10 times and my perspective has definitely changed. I have always been very critical of my hometown, about the school system, the job market (or lack of), and how the cloud of oppression seemed to hover over us heavier than the fog that covers Houston. I realized my view might have been skewed somewhat toward the negative because of my own personal views and experiences. I stopped one day to compare what the Jones's were doing, really examine how the neighbors had fared financially. Had they progressed? Were they still struggling financially? Or was my family's struggle based on my own stringent scale? In measuring progress, was I using the right criteria?

Should personal happiness count? What about one's ambition? I guess my dad has a disclaimer because of becoming disabled in his early forty's. In addition, my mom was a teenage bride that did not finish her education. As I ventured further and further away

217

from my hometown, I discovered people that had not finished their education nor had any formal training, but found financial success. Until recently, I hadn't realized how much poverty can affect a person—what it does to your self-esteem and your perspective on life. I found others doing well financially, others with better opportunities that forced me to take a closer look at my parent's decisions. I wanted to examine their maturation level, their goals and aspirations when they first started out. I did ask my dad once why he never left Alabama. After taking a moment to reflect, he thought of a couple of chances he'd had to relocate—to find better work. The first opportunity was passed over because he didn't want to leave his hometown. The second time my mom was afraid to leave. Fear halted their ambition. What was it to be so afraid of—failure, the unknown, the big city? Were they so afraid to leave their families or comfort level that they could not envision change as a positive or as a chance to make a better living for their children? It almost seemed better if I hadn't found out that the Joneses were achieving financial success. Then I might not have focused on what my family didn't have.

There are still times when the frustration levels run high from having to juggle so many needs with so little finances, but my parents are happy with their achievements. They are proud to be homeowners, and to have healthy, loving children. They have learned to appreciate the simple, non-tangibles things in life. I recognize that money was scarce, but do remember that love was plentiful. I could fall back on the love and encouragement and this would bring me through. My trip back home to see my brother was another time that I was able to fall back on my families' support. My dad and mom were very strict and enforced that I get an

education. I understand why they pushed me so hard now. They recognized their limitations and did not want me to bear the same burdens of constant financial struggles. After leaving my parent's home that Sunday morning, I realized it came to me. Perhaps I have become obsessed with my own desire for success and my own overwhelming ambitions that I had unreasonable expectations. Has my personal drive been perpetuated by memories of constant struggles and essential needs not met as a child? Has growing up as a "have-not" caused me to lose hope and become bitter? I know it has caused me to strive harder to reach my full potential. I have to credit my parents for bringing me to adulthood and I can't hold the choices they made for their lives against them. Instead I will learn from their life lessons as I journey through my life. With every challenge, I am now more appreciative and thankful for the assistance my parents did provide and it will not be forgotten.

Upon returning to Houston, I called daily to check on my brother. He was improving and getting strong as each week passed. Five weeks later, on May 23rd, on his 31st birthday, my brother was finally able to come home. He had to keep the tube in his side and wear a bag to drain the fluid for several more weeks. It took him two months to regain enough strength to do everyday tasks. This experience changed his life and my perspective. Before his illness, he was a very light hearted and carefree person. Now he is ready to take on responsibility and is very serious about life. The crisis of my brother Bruce becoming seriously ill gave me a chance to understand my family. I gained valuable knowledge from their wisdom and determination. No one knows how they will respond to a crisis, but my brother's illness helped me to realize the importance of family.

let Love LIVE
by Shirley Crews Taylor

My Brothers

When I am with my brothers, I feel such support and
about me they do not play
We have each others back, right or wrong so watch what you say
For the longest time I was the only girl and was out numbered so
I had to hold my own We played, we fought
and I had to stay strong
Our parents taught us to stick together and
to stay close and that we have done
The first two are right behind me and the
last two were young enough to be a son
Growing up, there was never a dull moment with us
When and if I need them I know I have their love, respect and
trust For my brothers there is nothing I would not do
They have been there for me and just know
I will always be there for them too
Even though one (Jamarcus) has passed, he is still in our heart
I pray daily for my brothers and nothing can tear us apart.
We now all have our own families and
do not always get to hang out
But if we need each other… we will be there without a doubt.

I am excited to share a story about the couple that lived on
Nicholson Street in Brent, Alabama. Mildred and DeAthur Crews
Sr, married on June 5, 1967. To this union a total of 7 children
were raised here, plus a host of others needing a place to stay.
Their house was an open door, and was always filled with people

coming in and out often. Mom was a great cook and dad loved to eat, so it worked out well. They did not have much, but always shared with others. There was always so much love and laughter. They were married for 48 years, and both passed in less than 2 months of each other in 2014 while in my care in Houston, Texas. This poem was of their 40th anniversary and vow renewal.

They're Still Together

The 40th Wedding Anniversary Of Dearthur
& Mildred Crews (June 5th 2006)

The Introduction

He remembers being in the church yard and asking,
"Who is that girl?"
He saw this pretty little thang and she rocked his world.
She said she met him when she was just 15 years old.
She was introduced to him by her cousin JV outside of New Oak
Grove. He said, "What's your name?"
and she said, "Pudding Tam, ask me again and
I will tell you the same."
He said, "Oh, you a fast little thang!"
He liked her the first time he saw her, it was love at first sight.
He couldn't wait to see her.
He went to her house that very same night.
She was attracted to him right away. She liked the way he made
everyone laugh, his jokes, and his play.

The Courtship

She introduced him to her parents, and he came down every
Sunday and stayed until 9pm.
She was smitten, the more they talked,
the more she wanted to see him.

by Shirley Crews Taylor

They wrote beautiful love letters from the day they met.
Poetic lines that were hard to forget.
Lines like, "Babe, my love for you makes the world go around."
"A love so strong makes a rabbit hug a hound."

The First Kiss

When asked about the first kiss, she claimed to
not remember the time or day.
He knew the time and place like it was yesterday.
He said, "It was 1965 in the backyard under the oak tree,
with sugar that sweet, she was the only one for me."

The Proposal

Time passed quickly, they became more serious and
talked about what the future would be.
While sitting on the couch, he asked her, "Will you marry me?"
She told him that he would have to ask her
dad and have him agree.
Her father was on his knees working on something the
day he asked for his daughter's hand.
Her father jumped straight up from what he was doing to
face him man to man.
He told him that he would think about it, and let him
know on the next Sunday.
Her father asked, "Are you really ready for this?"
She said, "Yes," and he didn't stand in their way.

by Shirley Crews Taylor

The Wedding

Their wedding day was June 5, 1966.
The planning was done, her mom made her dress,
and they were on their way.
About 40 to 50 people showed up on their wedding day.
Aunt Sennie was the maid of honor and
Uncle Skoochie was best man for dad.
They didn't have cake, only cookies and kool-aid,
a great time was had.
He put her in his car and drove her to Brent.
They moved in with Aunt Jessie, this is where their first three
months of marriage was spent.
They had only $12.00 between the two of them
on their first night.
But the love was there and their future was bright.

The Early Years

She said, "When they first got married they got
along well and understood each other."
|They would mostly eat, drink sodas,
and spend time with one another.
He didn't drink, smoke, or hang out with the bad boys.
He just stayed around the house.
They enjoyed going to the movies in
Selma and just being each other's spouse.

Let Love LIVE
by Shirley Crews Taylor

The Children

He had been asking for a baby.
One day he came home for lunch
and she told him that she thought she was pregnant.
They welcomed their baby girl, Shirley Ann:
On December 2nd, a cold and rainy Monday.
They were both very excited and not quite sure of what to say.
They welcomed DeArthur Jr about 1 ½ years later
On May 23rd, they had their first son.
Then on April 13th, exactly 11 months later,
Came Adam Demetrius, another one.
They took a break from having children and thought
they were done at three.
But only three children weren't meant to be.
Later came JaMarcus Dionne on April 5, 1983,
And Brian Lamar on November 11, 1985.
It's a real blessing to have healthy children that are all alive.
With five children already, when asked to take two more,
Most people would have said, "No way!"
But after Madear passed Tina and Marilyn
Became their daughters and a part of their family to stay.

The Years Between

He said there were bitter times and good times.
He had to give her space to grow.
They both had their wild times and the strain
on their marriage began to show.

by Shirley Crews Taylor

One day he decided it was time to settle down.
He stopped drinking, gambling, and all that running around.
He said when she would start fussing he would go outside
And let her cool off because the fighting didn't pay.
So most times he was the one to walk away.
When he got sick during the marriage, she stood by his side.
She worked hard and tried to provide.
He admired her for working hard and not throwing it in his face.
People would say there was nothing wrong with him.
But they made it through by God's grace.
When asked, "Why did she decide to hang in there?"
She said, "The children really loved their father and
the bond was always there."
After ten years with no job or income,
his disability finally started.
It was a great celebration after many years of disappointments
and being downhearted. He vowed to not let anyone talk to them
about their business or listen to hearsay.
"I didn't marry the people. I married you", he would say.
He knew he wouldn't find another woman that would put up
With the mess and the way he used to be.
She's been a good wife and I appreciate her.
She made a man out of me.

40 Years Later…

Lessons Learned & Words of Advice

I feel better now that we go to church every Sunday.
He loves the Lord and he loves his wife.
Blessed be the name of the Lord,
And with Mildred he wants to spend the rest of his life.
He loved her then and loves her better now than
the day they met, To death do us part.
We're still growing strong and she'll always have my heart.
They love their seven children and are proud of who they are.
It lets them know that they have done something right so far.
They enjoy life better now; 40 years have been like the first.
The key to a good marriage is having trust and understanding
For better or worse.
If you make a mistake, take the time to make it right.
Keep God as the head of your family
And he will be that guiding light.
Don't do anything that the other one doesn't know about.
Talk and decide on it together.
Work it out!
The flame burns even deeper, and their love will last forever.
After 40 years they are still together.

My Love for Sky

Accidentally releasing my pet bird still haunts me. Like a mother, I think I hear the sound of his voice. I never noticed as many birds or even looked up as much until I lost my budgie Sky. I still do not know how to forgive myself for trusting a bird to not do what birds do when outside. I still do not know what I was thinking. Again, like a mother with a toddler that cries when she leaves, I did not want to leave him. He was perched on my shoulder and refused to leave me. So, I decided to let him come with me for the walk to the mailbox. It was a terrible mistake. As soon as we got across the street, he seemed startled and took off. I panicked silently, embarrassed after being warned not to let him outside. I did not know what to do and I tried to stay calm. I continued my errand of checking the mail and then returned to see if I saw him. I have been walking outside for days looking up, blowing kissing sounds and yelling Sky. The neighbors are suspicious. But more than that, I can't stop kicking myself for what I have done. My heart aches and bleeds for him. The sound of other birds traumatizes me like the movie the birds did as a child. I never noticed how beautiful he was with his distinctive blue and gray colors. The little brown birds that taunt me daily do not compare.

See my bird Sky showed up to my home just like he left, out of nowhere. I first spotted him on my back deck, my dog tried to scare him away and then he flew into my kitchen window trying to escape. Only later to find him on my front porch. I kept going to the door to see if he was still there. After a couple of hours, I went to the store and bought him a cage and the rest they say is history.

That was 11 months ago. We became fast companions, I taught him lessons about how to say his name and I love you. Then I even taught him how to give me kisses and make kissy sounds. We were best buds and I even called him my guy Sky. My daughter said he was my emotional support animal. Until now, I didn't know that I needed one.

Family and friends were amazed with our bond. He had even learned to come to my office to find me. I never thought of myself as an animal person until he came along. I mean, we had dogs and I was kind. But the spiritual connection that I had with Sky was unparalleled like no other. My husband would even get jealous of the many kisses he would give me and how he would just nestle in my chest.

I have to find a way to move forward, to forgive myself for being careless and trusting with an animal that followed his instincts better than me. I even call out to him in my mind in hopes that he can hear me. One week out and I am inconsolable. Others suggest that I just go and buy another bird but for me there will never be another Sky.

My Love for Sky

One day to my surprise I spotted this beautiful
blue bird on my back deck
I brought it to my daughter's attention and it was not
what I would expect.
Just then my dog noticed him too
He started to bark and it startled the bird so he flew
He ran into the kitchen window and seemed to go away
But to our surprise he had gone to the front porch and there he
lay Like a child I was surprised by such a visit
I wondered why a bird was just hanging around like that,
I wondered what is it?
After an hour or two, I left to find a cage,
I said if he was still there when I got back
I would take him inside.
I went to the pet store and picked up a bird starter kit and called
to see if he was still there as I was returning from my ride
To my amazement he was still there so I brought him in
And this was the beginning of me and my wonderful friend
I would wake and look forward to cleaning
his cage as one of my chores
He never tried to escape or go through open doors
This gave me a false sense of security and I lowered my guard
I did not realize that losing my bird would be this hard.
We hung out daily and I even bought a carrier to take him on
trips He had such personality and a range of emotions

he learned to cuddle and actually kiss me on the lips
Months passed and he became a part of the family
and seemed as happy as could be
He brought such joy and happiness to me
Now it feels like a loss suddenly and there is no time to prepare
Who knew that for a bird, like this I would learn to care
Now I am sick with grief I tell you and
I do not wanna say goodbye
Another bird with never match the bond that I had with Sky
I pray that he is safe some place and maybe found his home
I would hate to think of him being in some tree all alone
But because Of my loss of sky, I am always looking
up and stopping near every tree
I have to trust that it was his destiny to roam and fly free.
I think no will always be looking over my shoulder in hope
Is that he might one day be together again
I am sorry that this was the way our story has to end
I love Sky… my man my man my man

For the People I Love

Today I was organizing my side of the room as things were starting to pile up (again)

I found expired medication, coins, old receipts, birthday cards, thank you cards from people I love. One birthday card had my actual age on it! I laughed and thought, the nerve! lol I found old boxes and envelopes from people that I love. I looked around the room and noticed a mound of personal artifacts that I thought, no one cares about these things but me. As I get older, I am realizing more and more that things do not bring me happiness but it's the memory or emotion that I feel for some of these things. Especially when I receive items from the people that I love.

As each year goes by, I find myself reflecting more and more about why I do what I do.

If I did not wake up, how soon would my family throw away my black box by my bed with the books and magazines that I intend to read. Or what about my favorite brown sandals with pearls? Then it hit me that it would not matter. That death is the ultimate surrender and loss of control. I am not ashamed to admit that I struggle with ego and having boundaries. Some days I think I need to hang on and sometimes I want to let it all go, but what and when? I am sure this whole message is what others describe as a "random" thought. I agree, but this time I am documenting the madness because I feel that there is a lesson here somewhere. Looking over my things and the material things that I have been able to amass in this life thus far, I think of my mother.

It was not until her last year that I learned things about her that I did the same thing and was not aware of until she got sick and had to move out of her home and stay with me. I was going through her personal items when I discovered this beautiful red box. When I saw it, I instantly knew that it was empty and why she had held on to it. It wasn't to repurpose it, it was simply because she thought it was beautiful and that it was a gift from someone she loved. I always did the same thing. When she passed, I found things that she had never opened or used. Again, I did the same thing. It made me realize that there were so many powerful lessons that I learned from my mother's life. I finally understood her. I made a commitment to enjoy the beautiful things that the people I loved had given me and that it was ok to have the "wants" and desires of my own heart.

I still catch myself storing the nice things away. So today, I will commit to using the pretty glass, to burn that good candle. I am also willing to release the envelope and the beautiful box (well some of them! Hey it's a process) I also learned in my mother's death that I was not living fully, but just sacrificing myself for others. Now, with years of growth and healing, I can say today that I am focusing on life and thriving. I am grateful.

So as I declutter today, and reflect on my journey thus far…I am so thankful.

I am thankful for the many lessons my mom taught me. I am choosing to live a vibrant life with a full array of emotions. I am eating the cake, using my good china and feeling whatever comes up from my spirit.

by Shirley Crews Taylor

I wrote this poem in closing and in dedication to the people I love. They have helped to shape me and see the many facets of myself and for that, I am appreciative. I hope you can understand why you do what you do, especially for the people that you love.

For The People I Love

I think I was born to be a nurturer and to care
deeply was a natural gift
My purpose has been to encourage those with broken hearts and
spirits that needed a lift
My position as the oldest child and daughter really
shaped and molded me.
My mom and her mom had the same position you see
She had to be a mom-daughter and she raised me the same way
I catch myself reminding myself that I am only
the sister even to this day
For the people I love I could show up with a smile
I provided active listening , a helpful hand and went the extra
mile It seems for a time, I had run out of gas
I had poured too much from my cup from my past
For the people that I love, there has been nothing
for them that I would not do
I have given my time my money my all
to prove my love was true
I do not blame anyone for the things that
I have done and the path taken on this route
Somewhere the messages and values told me
to give my all until my all was out

let
Love
LIVE

by Shirley Crews Taylor

For the people I love, I have devoted my time and
it was a great distraction
It kept me from working on my stuff and
to do the work I would not take action
The taste of resentment and bitterness became great
But I am thankful I was able to make the required
changes before it was too late
Now, as I reflect upon this, I must admit it might
sound like a sad story
But for the people I love, I have no regrets and
I give God the glory.
Because the lessons I learned, I will not have to take them again
To the people I love, I will strive to be a better person and
continue to give love until the end.

Domestic Violence Against Women (1998)

Domestic violence affects everyone in all walks of life. You may have a mother or know someone that has a sister or female cousin that is being abused or have lost their lives at the hands of someone they loved. According to FBI statistics, 30% of female murder victims were killed by their husbands or boyfriends. One-third of all female homicide victims are killed by husbands, ex-husbands, boyfriends or ex-boyfriends. Almost four (4) million American women were physically abused by their partners in the last year alone. But this social issue is more than statistics for me, it takes on more of a personal meaning as a woman and being a member of the African-American community. Mary Jean Crews died in June, 1979 on Fathers Day. She was shot to death by her live-in boyfriend, Dave James outside a club in Brent, Alabama.

I can remember being awake in the early morning hours for some reason, I can't recall now. Then there were several quick, hard knocks at the front door and a man's voice yelled "DeArthur! Dave shot Jean and they think she's dead!!!"

My dad was my aunt Jean's big brother and the one everyone came running to when something bad happened. I can remember my dad jumping up and getting dressed hurriedly. I asked to go with him, but he refused. I sat out on the front porch and waited for my dad to return. The radio was playing , I don't know who turned it on,

but the song on the radio was called "Funky Town". It played over and over again in my

head..."won't you take me to Funky Town...won't you take me to Funky town!" It stayed embedded in my head for years to come and when I would hear it I would think of that summer night. The night was so quiet with the exception of this song that seemed to play forever. I can remember feeling very comfortable on what had been a hot, sultry day.

There was a soft breeze that left you feeling like you could sit there always. Everything was happening in slow motion. It would be several hours before my dad returned. While I waited, I began to think about my aunt Jean and how special she was to me. I can remember her always being so sweet to me. She was patient, often calling me baby, "yes baby...you can do it baby...okay baby".

Aunt Jean had five (5) children, one son, four daughters and another one on the way. She had a deep rich laugh and a smile so big, you couldn't help but feel loved by her. She was a beautiful woman to me. She wasn't very tall, but had big hips and a small waist. She had the prettiest legs and would always wear stacked hill sandals with the back out. My aunt was loud and country. She loved hard and fought hard.

At the time, Aunt Jean's youngest daughter was only one and she had a knee baby who was two years old. I hadn't stopped to think what their lives would be like without her. I couldn't imagine my aunt being taken away from us so soon. My dad returned and confirmed my worst nightmare-Aunt Jean had been killed and it was Dave who had shot her while her kids were home in bed sleeping.

How could this happen? My young mind struggled to comprehend. Dave was supposed to love her! They were always together. As the news of my aunt Jean's murder began to sink in, I don't remember going back to bed that fathers day eve.

Dave James was arrested, jailed and released in six (6) months. I was so young, I couldn't understand how a man could kill someone (my aunt!) and not be punished. I'm still not sure why he didn't go to prison for his crime. It was rumored that because my grandmother's failure to press charges ultimately set him free. The events leading up to her death had left subtle clues of the potential for something this devastating happening. I recall, as a little girl, overhearing my aunt and her boyfriend in an argument. I had stayed overnight with my cousins and Aunt Jean and Dave were in the bedroom arguing. I can remember my cousin pleading with my aunt, saying "Jean please don't fight", "Jean please don't fight." She called her mom by her first name for some reason. Dave was always jealous of my aunt, being so particular about what she could wear or where she could go. But who would have imagined the situation would have escalated to murder. The witnesses say that my aunt Jean approached Dave and another woman-this was what led to the violent encounter. My dad lost his baby sister, I lost my aunt in the prime of her life and her five(5) children lost their mother to a senseless act of violence.

Most domestic violence go unnoticed because others keep silent and many of us just don't want to get involved. I wrote a poem entitled, "Stop The Silence!!!", hoping it will help increase community awareness. It goes as follows:

by Shirley Crews Taylor

Stop The Silence

(In Loving Memory of Mary Jean Crews)

One hot night a man filled with rage and aggression--
not thinking of anyone but himself committed a terrible
transgression!
In a heated argument, shot and killed his girlfriend:
What a tragic way so many women's lives seem to end.
He didn't stop to think how destructive it would be to
kill a mother of five;
or how nothing else could be done to bring her back alive!
This beautiful person, even a mother to be!
She was someone's daughter, a sister and an aunt to me.
I can remember the night we got this frantic knock at the door,
a man yelled, "Dave shot Jean, and they think she's dead";
My father (her brother) jumped out of bed!
I waited on the porch for him to return;
This would be the hardest lesson I would have to learn.
Why a man could take such
a wonderful life in a cold, heartless way;
And how the justice system would have little to say.
I was only 12 at the time and could not fully understand;
How this man would eventually go free to walk this land.
They said it was because my grandmother
would not press charges or take a stand...
But why would she need to if a grown woman
was killed by a grown man?

let **Love** LIVE
by Shirley Crews Taylor

So many women die from the hands of
someone they love and fear;
The statistics in the U.S. keep rising year after year;
But my aunt wasn't a number to me;
She was a person filled with positivity!
She had a smile so big, you couldn't help
but feel the love from her when she came around;
She always found a way to make me feel
better when I was down.
Like so many other women, maybe
she made a choice that was bad;
By loving a man that would eventually
kill her because he was mad.
I hope this poem will bring more attention to
domestic violence;
And encourage people to get involved and to
stop the silence!!! (1998)

Unfortunately, there is another side to this social issue that relates
to the serious problem we have in our community-especially the
black community of men going to prison for violent crimes. Some
people don't look at domestic violence as a crime, but there are
rising numbers of men going to prison for domestic abuse. F o r
almost two decades, the criminal justice system in the United
States has been undergoing a tremendous expansion. There are a
disproportionate number of Black men involved in the criminal
justice system. Research shows that almost one in four Blacks in
the age group 20 to 29 is either in prison, jail or on probation.
For Whites in this age group the numbers are one in 16 and for

Hispanics it's one in 10. Several of them commit different types of crimes, but domestic violence crimes tend to bring about a jail term as a last resort. These crimes often go unpunished because people keep silent.

For the Black community in general, nearly one fourth of its young men are under the control of the criminal justice system at the time when their peers are beginning families, learning constructive life skills, and starting careers. The consequences of this situation for family and community stability will be increasingly debilitating. Addressing the conditions which lead to domestic violence in the first place is a broad agenda which requires serious thought, attention and action. The problem of domestic violence as a crime is a complex one and will not be resolved overnight. By continuing to bring attention to this problem to our community and the society as a whole, we can make some changes that will save our mothers and sisters from being killed and our brothers and fathers from being lost to jail terms. Every October local programs, state coalitions and national organizations conduct community awareness campaigns, fund-raisers and special events to educate the public about the problem of domestic violence and its effect on the victims and community at large.

In conclusion, I want to share another poem I wrote about a domestic violence situation that happened just outside my bedroom window. I hope someone will be touched enough to start thinking about how we can make a difference on the social problem of domestic violence against women and the high rate of men going to prison. Communities are deeply affected by the loss of lives from murders and incarcerations-especially in the Black community. It goes as follows:

Another One Lost

He beat a woman they said;
Broke her nose and hit her in the head.
The officers, White, dressed in Blue;
The man, Black, and it was true.
Little boy, (the man's son),
just stood there as they arrested his father,
His friends beside him, none of them seemed to bother.
It broke my heart as I watched from my apartment window;
To know a man beat a helpless woman,
and no regret he seems to show. To see a black man get arrested
and to have the young black boys to see;
I had to step away, because it really got to me.
Tears came to my eyes and fear to my heart;
Because the trends keep setting-it's tearing our lives apart.
As they through him on in their car, he waved to his
son one last time- somehow finding a smile;
knowing what he had done, he would be gone a while.
Another Black man lost from society, and gone to jail;
What's the price this time and who signs the bail?
How long will this type of thing last?
It has followed us into our future from our rocky past.
People, it's time to make a change, just one of us or two:
Maybe a good example will help the others know what to do.
Don't let our men be lost;
And a poor, inefficient society is the cost!
By: Shirley Crews Taylor (1988)

let
Love
LIVE
by Shirley Crews Taylor

I wrote a love letter to Galveston, Texas after hearing a sports commentator speak negatively about Galveston. I was appalled by the way it called Galveston's water dirty and that it was not a "real" beach. I was late to the game in discovering my Galveston, but I got here as soon as I could. I love to be in love with the idea of love. In my creativity, I wanted to show my love and affection to the city of Galveston, Texas as if this city was a person. So I pinned a love letter to Galveston.

Galveston has been my safe place and a huge part of my healing process. When I would visit the ocean it reminded me how small I am in the overall scheme of things. I am in awe of what God created and how good it has been to me. I hope you will enjoy my letters to Galveston both part one and part two. It allowed me to be creative and explore my hopeless romantic ideals:

let
Love
LIVE
by Shirley Crews Taylor

A Love Letter to My Galveston

Galveston —My Confidant …My Refuge

I have finally found a place and someone where
I can be myself and fully release
He accepts me just as I am, no judgment only peace
I often show up exhausted and drained
His winds and fresh air eases my pain
My thoughts rush to me and I can hear them clearly as
I put footprints in his sand He caresses my soul and
with him I can go for activities or not have a plan
He lets me takes his sea shells and feel the waves from his ocean
He calms me down and takes me away
from all the worldly commotion
After my walk then I always stop by Goodwill
He knows where I go each time to get a cheap thrill
When I am hungry he feeds me and allows me to shop
All my fears, stress and worries he lets me drop
He is not selfish with my time and he lets
me come and go as I please
The love and kindness he provides me I always feel his warmth
no matter the degrees
With him time seems to stop while watching sunsets or
the rising moon takes my breath away
I leave him each time renewed no matter how long I stay

let Love LIVE

by Shirley Crews Taylor

Whenever I return he never disappoints and makes
me feel right at home
Things have gotten so serious that to be close
to him I bought my own place
I rent it out when I am not there and really enjoy the space
He builds my confidence and with him I never feel alone
To others, Galveston, Texas is not a big deal but for me he's huge
I will be forever in love and devoted to my "Galveston",
my confidant and my refuge.

let
Love
LIVE
by Shirley Crews Taylor

A letter to My Galveston Part II -He knows I'm for the Beach (Streets!)

I feel like I cheated on my Galveston, because I recently took
a few cruises to Mexico then the Bahamas, and the water was great
The time was wonderful, I enjoyed another body of water,
including the rest and all the food I ate
The water was so nice that I could not turn away.
I was out on the balcony just staring at this body
of water every day
Now I know that me and my Galveston had
a special thing going on
But I never thought I could step out so easily and
it feels guilty and wrong
I fell into lust for those strong waves and that beautiful aqua blue
Before I knew it, I was going back again and
I forgot about me and you (My Galveston)
I am thankful for the time and rendezvous with other beaches,
he I knew it would not last
When I returned to my Galveston, he said that we did not have to
speak on it, and it was all in the past
With my Galveston, no lies I had to tell or excuses I had to make
He took me back with open arms and forgave my every mistake
I know I was disrespectful and our agreement I did breach
But he understands me and knows that I am for the beach

Reflection Page
Chapter 7

_____

_____

_____

_____

_____

_____

_____

_____

_____

Prayers and Bible Verses

This chapter is a gentle nudge from my Aunt Daisey to "talk about God". I have always had a big heart and loved hard and deeply. With a big heart and loving deeply brings heartache and disappointments. I have learned to lean not on my own physical strength, but to believe in a higher power. I am not here to convert anyone else or change what others think. I am finally using my voice to share my beliefs and what I think, as well as what has helped me to personally heal and grow. I have included a few prayers that I often go to and verses that have helped me to stand on what God says about me and his promises when I feel weak, unworthy, and not loved or bold. As I continue to "Let Love Live", I am amazed and in awe of what God has done in my life. Breaking me in areas I did not understand and healing me in ways I could not have imagined for my life. Take what you need from my words and leave the rest. In closing, finally, "I said what I said-unapologetically!" I love you. Be blessed.

let
Love
LIVE
by Shirley Crews Taylor

Chapter Eight: Prayers and Verses
Prayers

The Lord's Prayer	Prayer For Sick Child	Prayer For Mother
Our Father which art in heaven, Hallowed be thy name. Thy kingdom come, Thy will be done in earth, as it is in heaven. Give us this day our daily bread. And forgive us our debts, as we forgive our debtors. And lead us not into temptation, but deliver us from evil; For thine is the kingdom, and the power, and the glory, A-men. Matthew 6:9-13	Father thank you for my child: If it's for a lifetime or only for a while. Lord, let me know what I need to do; To raise my child in the likeness of you; Take away any thoughts I have that is not your will; Give our child relief from any pain he or she may feel. Bless our family and give us faith that will last; Let us remember that this too shall pass. *Amen.*	Lord, even though our mother has passed away; We want to show our appreciation on this special day. Mother, the pictures of your smile still shine bright; The memories of you have been our guiding light. It wasn't easy having children to raise; We thank God for you and we give him praise. You were the glue that kept the family together— We will be grateful forever. Although we wish you could be here; But know you are in our hearts and always near. Amen.

Bible Verses

James 1:2 "My brothers and sisters, think of the various tests you encounter as occasions for joy"

James 1:4 "But you must learn to endure everything, so you will be completely mature and not lacking in anything"

Ephesians 4:30 "Don't make the Holy Spirit of God unhappy— you were sealed by him for the day of redemption."

Romans 15:13 "May the God of hope fill you with all joy and peace in faith so that you overflow with hope by the power of the Holy Spirit."

Matthew 11:28 "Come to me, all you who are struggling hard and carrying heavy loads, and I will give you rest."

Psalms 34:18 34:19 "The LORD is close to the brokenhearted; he saves those whose spirits are crushed." "The righteous have many problems, but the LORD delivers them from every one."

Romans 8:18, 8:28 "I believe that the present suffering is nothing compared to the coming glory that is going to be revealed to us." "We know that God works all things together for good for the ones who love God, for those who are called according to his purpose."

Philippians 4:12,13 "I know the experience of being in need and of having more than enough; I have learned the secret to being

by Shirley Crews Taylor

content in any and every circumstance, whether full or hungry or whether having plenty or being poor." "I can endure all these things through the power of the one who gives me strength."

Romans 12:2 "Don't be conformed to the patterns of this world, but be transformed by the renewing of your minds so that you can figure out what God's will is—what is good and pleasing and mature."

Romans 3:23, 24 "All have sinned and fall short of God's glory," "but all are treated as righteous freely by his grace because of a ransom that was paid by Christ Jesus."

John 16:33 "I've said these things to you so that you will have peace in me. In the world you have distress. But be encouraged! I have conquered the world. "

James 1:1-4 "Let this endurance complete its work so that you may be fully mature, complete, and lacking in nothing."

John 4:16 "We have known and have believed the love that God has for us. God is love, and those who remain in love remain in God and God remains in them."

Ephesians 6:10 "Finally, be strengthened by the Lord and his powerful strength."

Philippians 4: 6,7 "Don't be anxious about anything; rather, bring up all of your requests to God in your prayers and petitions, along with giving thanks." "Then the peace of God that exceeds

all understanding will keep your hearts and minds safe in Christ Jesus."

Romans 12:2 "Don't be conformed to the patterns of this world, but be transformed by the renewing of your minds so that you can figure out what God's will is—what is good and pleasing and mature."

Proverbs 4:23 "More than anything you guard, protect your mind, for life flows from it."

James 1:4 "Let this endurance complete its work so that you may be fully mature, complete, and lacking in nothing."

Isaiah 41:10 "Don't fear, because I am with you; don't be afraid, for I am your God. I will strengthen you, I will surely help you; I will hold you with my righteous strong hand."

Galatians 5:22,23 "But the fruit of the Spirit is love, joy, peace, patience, kindness, goodness, faithfulness," "gentleness, and self-control. "There is no law against things like this."

Romans 12:12 "Be happy in your hope, stand your ground when you're in trouble, and devote yourselves to prayer."

Matthew 6:31-33 "Therefore, don't worry and say, 'What are we going to eat?' or 'What are we going to drink?' or 'What are we going to wear?'" "Gentiles long for all these things. Your heavenly Father knows that you need them." "Instead, desire first and foremost God's kingdom and God's righteousness, and all these things will be given to you as well."

Nahum 1:7 "The LORD is good, a haven in a day of distress. He acknowledges those who take refuge in him."

Hebrews 11:6 "It's impossible to please God without faith because the one who draws near to God must believe that he exists and that he rewards people who try to find him."

II Corinthians 4:8 "We are experiencing all kinds of trouble, but we aren't crushed. We are confused, but we aren't depressed."

John 16:33 "I've said these things to you so that you will have peace in me. In the world you have distress. But be encouraged! I have conquered the world. "

II Corinthians 5-7 "We live by faith and not by sight."

I Peter 2:24 "He carried in his own body on the cross the sins we committed. He did this so that we might live in righteousness, having nothing to do with sin. By his wounds you were healed."

2 Timothy 4:10, 7 "Demas has fallen in love with the present world and has deserted me and has gone to Thessalonica. Crescens has gone to Galatia, and Titus has gone to Dalmatia."

Ester 4:14 "In fact, if you don't speak up at this very important time, relief and rescue will appear for the Jews from another place, but you and your family will die. But who knows? Maybe it was for a moment like this that you came to be part of the royal family."

Isaiah 55: 8,9 "My plans aren't your plans, nor are your ways my ways, says the LORD." "Just as the heavens are higher than the

earth, so are my ways higher than your ways, and my plans than your plans."

Jeremiah 29:11-13 (NIV) "For I know the plans I have for you," declares the Lord, "plans to prosper you and not to harm you, plans to give you hope and a future. Then you will call on me and come and pray to me, and I will listen to you. You will seek me and find me when you seek me with all your heart."

1 PETER 5:7, NLT "Give all your worries and cares to God, for he cares about you."

Reflection Page
Chapter 8

_____

_____

_____

_____

_____

_____

_____

_____

_____

_____

About The Author

Shirley Crews Taylor has been writing poetry since she was a child. She is a poet, author, coach, and consultant.

Shirley has a unique ability to make a deep connection with others in an authentic way. She also has a true gift for expressing the hearts of others through words as it comes easily for her. Shirley enjoys experiencing the emotional responses that her poetry generates for the recipient of the gift. Her writing has been known to evoke tears of joy.

She owns and operates SAC Creations, a division of her company TCT Enterprises, LLC. Our services strives to assist businesses and individuals with thoughtful and unique ways share with others how much they are valued.

Her products and services are designed to promote encouragement and display appreciation, while also providing a beautiful keepsake that will last for years to come.

Shirley assists customers with expressing the feelings flowing from the heart.